THE WHOLE Organic FOOD BOOK

Safe, Healthy Harvest
from Your Garden
to Your Plate

Dan Jason

RAINCOAST BOOKS
Vancouver

Raincoast Books acknowledges the ongoing support of the Government of Canada through the Book Publishing Industry Development Program (BPIDP).

First published in 2001 by

Raincoast Books
9050 Shaughnessy Street
Vancouver, B.C. Canada
V6P 6E5

www.raincoast.com

1 2 3 4 5 6 7 8 9 10

NATIONAL LIBRARY OF CANADA
CATALOGUING IN PUBLICATION DATA

Jason, Dan.
 The whole organic food book

 Includes bibliographical references.
 ISBN 1-55192-426-9

 1. Organic gardening. 2. Cookery (Natural foods)
I. Title.
SB453.5.J39 2001   635'.0484   C2001-910262-3

Cover and text design by Gabi Proctor/DesignGeist

Printed and bound in Canada

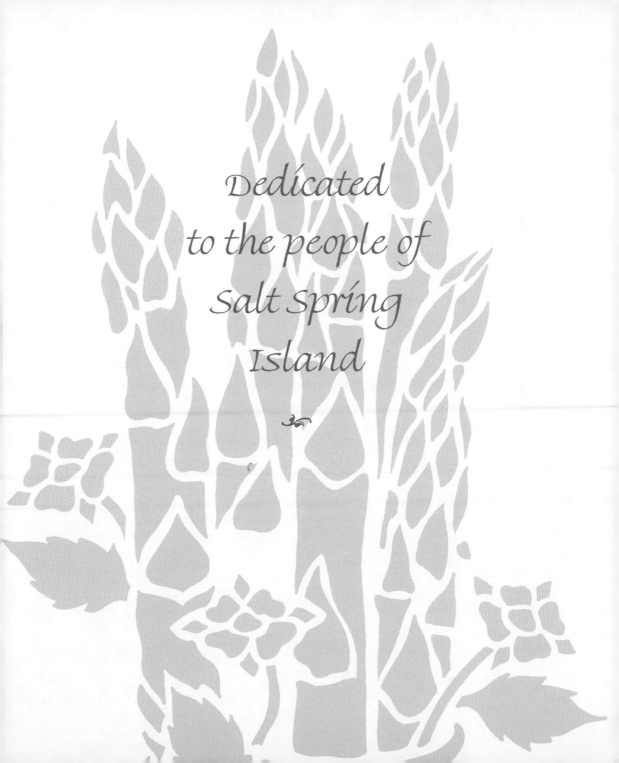

Dedicated
to the people of
Salt Spring
Island

Contents

Foreword

Something dangerous is being done to the food we eat, something that has never been done in 10,000 years of growing food on this planet. Our food is being bio-engineered with genes from many other life forms and it is being presented to us without identification and with almost no examination of possible consequences. The first genetically modified foods were approved in the early 1990s and now, less than a decade later, it is almost impossible to buy processed foods without genetically modified components. Our governments aggressively support transnational corporations in their bid to limit our food choices to their corporate creations.

"Organic" is, of course, only a word, but it is quickly becoming an extremely important word that stands for the alternative to gene-tinkered foods. In 1998, the U.S. Department of Agriculture tried to include genetically modified (GM) foods in the definition of "organic." Word got out over the internet, and close to 300,000 people protested. In the fast shuffling that is now going on over regulations governing certified organic food, organic is taking on a more powerful identification than ever. Its equation with non-GM crops is already overshadowing its essential earlier meanings.

The principles and practices of organic growing have always honoured natural processes and a living Earth. I hope this book provides insight and inspiration for those wanting to grow and/or eat organic food.

In discussing issues raised by genetically engineered food, this book anticipates an even greater increase in popularity for organic agriculture, which has been growing by 30 percent yearly for almost a decade. There is a rapidly accelerating belief that "organic" is a place where people can take a stand and truly make a difference. It has been quite impossible for the ordinary person to do anything about the loss of clean air, earth and water, but we can vote with our food dollars and gardeners' hands to keep our food healthy.

There's no mistaking that the issue of food is a gigantic one and that the powers that be are going all out to gain the kind of control that puts them in our mouths at every meal, every day. In essence a battle is shaping up as people realize that to go organic is to not buy into the

mindless and heartless destruction of the Earth. Food, because it is so basic, may be the one arena where a sense of public trust can be rekindled and then spread to other aspects of society.

Whole food goes hand in hand with organic and safe food these days because it is still possible to grow and obtain vegetables, fruits, nuts, beans and grains that are not contaminated by foreign genes. Eating low on the food chain is definitely the way to go if you wish to abstain from Frankenfoods. Whole beans and grains especially have the capacity to become the mainstay of our diets. I hope this book conveys to you the exciting and surprising wealth of possibilities in beans and grains. I encourage you to learn of their delights by growing even small amounts of them and to support organic growers in their efforts to provide us with such nutritious, diverse and resource-efficient foods. I hope the recipes show how simple and satisfying it is to prepare the beans and grains that can grow where we live.

One of the main points of this book is that there are absolutely no problems with the foods that have been handed down to us by our forebears. Contrary to corporate opinion, nature is already as abundant and glorious as all get-out and can fulfill our needs in the best possible ways. We have been losing our heritage of seeds at a staggering rate as we've become accustomed to "convenience" foods grown and processed with chemicals and poisons. The onslaught of genetically modified seeds, patented seeds and seeds that self-destruct makes it clear that we will soon have no seeds at all in the public domain if we don't act now. Awareness of the issues is crucial, as is support for organic gardening and agriculture. Active preservation of our tried-and-true seeds is also crucial, because we cannot rely on governments or corporations to have our best interests at heart. This book encourages you to participate in some innovative and exciting strategies for keeping our seeds alive.

May all be well fed.

Dan Jason
Salt Spring Island, B.C.

Introduction

I grew up in a large city, I have no background or training in agriculture and I've never owned a farm. Yet my experiences in working a couple of small acreages for the past 14 years have given me a special and privileged perspective on food and food growing. I've come to know, from the pleasure of doing it, that we could be feeding ourselves in a saner, healthier and happier way than we are doing at present.

Those two small farms that came under my stewardship, seemingly by chance, taught me that it is easily possible for a family to grow all its own food and find contentment on a half hectare of land. With a similar absence of planning, my creation of a mail-order seed company showed me that it is especially easy to succeed if you grow a diversity of crops.

This introduction is the short version of how I came to promote a safe and sustainable agriculture and to wish that other people could luck out like me and live on a small farm.

In the beginning, I was a transplanted city person and elementary school teacher with a small backyard garden. My career as an ardent gardener began in the early 1980s when the acreage across the road from me on Salt Spring Island (the largest of British Columbia's Gulf Islands) was purchased by a group of "off-islanders." The land quickly came to be called the Salt Spring Centre, a fitting name for a yoga, retreat and meditation facility in the heart of the island.

Thanks to no one else's wanting the job, I soon became the centre's head gardener. Just under one hectare of rich bottomland and a budget that enabled me to purchase seeds, supplies and equipment provided a challenging opportunity to grow food for large numbers of people. Meals were vegetarian, so I researched and grew crops that were high-protein foods capable of rounding out a diet rich in fruits and vegetables.

My first major discovery was a soybean called Black Jet that matured easily in the growing conditions at the Centre. Until then, I'd had disappointing experiences cooking whole soybeans. The Black Jets, though, tasted great with minimal seasoning and caused no indigestion for me or others. At the same time, I grew varieties of pinto, chili, soup and baking beans that were more delicious than any I had purchased from stores.

I was not only trying out various beans but also testing grains that would be appropriate for a kitchen garden. Two crops that stood out hail from South America. Amaranth and quinoa are gorgeous, drought-tolerant plants with a high yield that make very filling and satisfying meals.

When I started Salt Spring Seeds in 1986, listing some of my beans and grains in a mail-order seed catalogue, I was starting to feel that I was really onto something. I sensed that North Americans were beginning to shift to a more plant-based diet, yet our growing habits had not caught up. For example, billions of bushels of soybeans are grown annually for export, animal feed or processing, but hardly any are grown for direct human consumption.

Indeed, I was in the right place at the right time. Our seeds have been finding their way around the globe. Amaranth, quinoa and black soybeans have become commercial crops. Recipes for them and other "new" protein-rich plants have become standard in vegetarian cookbooks.

Soybeans, quinoa, beans and amaranth made for plenty of inspiration, but I also discovered lentils, favas, chick-peas, wheat, peas and barley. All are grown on a large scale in North America, but mostly for processing into food products or for export elsewhere. This seemed amazing to me, since many varieties of these are delicious cooked just as they are — simple, whole foods. Multiple revelations made my garden harvests sparkle with newness: there are pea cultivars that make fine soup peas and don't have to be split; there are barleys with hulls that easily rub off and don't have to be pearled; there are old wheat varieties, such as kamut and spelt, that many people with wheat allergies can tolerate.

After seven years at the Salt Spring Centre, I was invited by a friend, Ross McLeod, to share his space at Mansell Farm and to further pursue my growing experiments. I've now seen seven harvests at Mansell Farm, and three features of beans and grains have remained consistent. They are very easy to grow; they can produce a lot of food in a small area; they offer an incredible array of tastes and textures.

The recipes in this book highlight some of the easy and interesting ways I've found to prepare beans and grains. Like most North American kids, I grew up on a meat and dairy diet. It's been a gradual transition for me to so-called fibre foods, finding out over many years that they needn't be bland or boring. Twenty years ago I knew and appreciated dozens of cheeses, wines and cuts of meat, but never thought there'd be diverse, delightful and delectable surprises in beans and grains.

I found cooking with whole foods to be a refreshing and liberating activity that didn't require batters, doughs or exotic ingredients. The simplicity of whole foods calls for simple additions. Cooking beans and grains involves simmering them until they're done. Then it's a straightforward matter of adding dressings, sauces or sautés, or even enjoying their unadorned wholeness. Nor do you have to mess with greasy pans or packaging that deceptively identifies itself as "Part of a Simple Lifestyle."

A trip to Ethiopia in 1993 greatly broadened my perspective on whole foods. Ethiopians have farmed their land for as long as anyone on this Earth, and over 80 percent of them are still farmers. They grow most of the same crops I've cultivated and their farms are similar in size. As is true in many agrarian cultures in temperate climates, a hectare provides enough food to feed a large extended family. I was struck by the vibrant health of both the Ethiopian people and their agricultural land, dispelling the false expectations our media had created for me.

I returned to Salt Spring Island with a vision of 20 percent of North Americans growing our food instead of the two percent who do now. And I'm still promoting that vision, which gets more compelling all the time.

Growing food is a wonderful vocation that works best for everyone when growers maintain intimacy with what they cultivate. Large-scale, high-input agriculture has appeared to work because there was lots of good soil around when it began. But look at what's happened after only 50 years. Our soil and water are so depleted and polluted that there is precious little time to turn things around. To grow foods such as those featured in

this book, using methods that improve rather than destroy the land's health, to my mind is the sane way to go.

The notion of organic gardening is not such a radical one when you consider that it's mostly about being in touch with what's going on. The notion of eating whole grains and beans is not such a radical one, either, when you remember that such fare has sustained cultures all over the globe. As few as two or three of these foods have formed the staple diets of huge groups of people. We now have the opportunity to enjoy a great many of these crops and to celebrate a diet and an agriculture unprecedented in health-bestowing diversity.

Beans and grains are not only whole foods, they are seeds. As such they join the past and future, carrying the dream of a planet where all live in peace, health and joy. Corporate agriculture's current pursuit, trying to make all seeds proprietary, terminates in termination. I'm saying, "Let's go for the glory."

Organic Methods of Growing

I n my first days as a gardener, in the early 1980s, I never thought of my methods as "organic." I started to wonder about the term when a few visitors to the Salt Spring Centre garden insisted that formulations of chemical fertilizer were no less organic than the compost I used.

The garden had a slope and a flat area and to me the crucial thing was when and where to plant the seeds. The soil was rich and things grew if you helped them get ahead of the weeds. Besides compost, I added seaweed and dolomite lime, mulched, hoed, weeded and rotated crops in a sensible sort of way. It was all rather natural and … well … um … yes, organic.

Even now I have friends who, as I did back then, garden quite naturally and organically and don't bother with definitions.

But as I began to call myself a seed company it became increasingly important to have my own take on organic gardening and to tell people where I stood. I started writing magazine articles and even began a local chapter of Canadian Organic Growers. I came to see that the lines dividing organic and non-organic were often quite blurry. I'd like to give a couple of examples to illustrate the difficulties involved in making hard-and-fast rules about what is organically okay.

Organic certification associations stress the importance of rotating crops every year to prevent the buildup of pests and diseases. I learned quickly, however that crop yields increase significantly if you plant members of the same bean family in the same spot for two or three years. Tomatoes also like reinhabiting the same piece of ground. The question is: who decides what's okay?"

Organic-information sources present a lot of strategies for dealing with slugs, some of which are barriers and some traps. But there are no admonitions about killing slugs. The slugs at the Salt Spring Centre garden were abundant and voracious. My method of keeping their numbers down was to patrol in the predawn hours and snip them with a pair of scissors. I did this for several years until I decided it was a pretty nasty thing to be doing. I switched to transporting them in buckets to a considerable distance away.

So where does one draw the line about life and death in the garden and what's organically acceptable? Is it better to kill slugs and bugs directly, use organically acceptable pesticides, or get other bugs to do it? (The latter, called integrated pest management, is now an important organic pest management strategy.)

You must decide. Organic growers are always learning and organic gardening is a process of attunement that moves in the direction of what affirms life and works best.

The organic movement is clear that genetically modified seeds and crops are not in the best interests of anyone except those making money from them. What is not so clear for certified organic producers is how to protect the organic integrity of their crops from genetically modified organisms (GMOs). Organic certifiers require that no GMO or GMO derivatives be used in fertilizers, soil conditioners or plant protection, as seeds or vegetative production materials, as ingredients or processing aids, et cetera. This becomes a daunting task when GMO products are not even required to be labelled as such!

At the end of this section I outline the rapidly accelerating GMO pollution with which the organic producer must contend. Now, more than ever, organic certification groups need strong support in their difficult task of safeguarding our food.

I've had my issues with organic certification over the years. Like many farmers, I don't relish a lot of bureaucratic paperwork. I probably would never have become certified if my friend Camelia Frieberg hadn't completed the original application for me.

Some of my concerns have been broad ones. I used to think that organic methods didn't address "sustainable" choices very well. I've also seen organic farms getting larger and larger until they begin to resemble monoculture factory farms. As they've done so, it's become more important to address workers' rights in the context of organic farming.

However, I've come to appreciate the importance and necessity of a third-party certification process that people can trust and I've observed the healthy evolution of the organic movement in response to the challenges of an increasingly complex food system.

How important is it that organic food be certified? I think that it is, indeed, a matter of trust. Most people who buy organic food have no direct knowledge of how it was grown and for them a certified organic identification is the only way to be safe. But if you obtain your food from a friend or neighbour or through a box program that encourages you to visit the farm that supplies you, then it is both possible and desirable to assess whether everything is done in accordance with organic standards and your own. If you can trust your grower through a direct connection, then certification can become redundant.

Can organics feed the planet? Based on my own knowledge and experience, I say yes, yes and again yes. The naysayers of the world's giant agrichemical conglomerates say we have to splice fish genes into tomatoes, spray the countryside with poisonous chemicals and pour on chemical fertilizers if the world is to be fed. I say it's already too obvious that if we follow that path the world will be dead.

A reconnection with the natural order of things is greatly needed at this time. The Earth has grown inhospitable toward human presence as we have ceased to recognize the sacred character of habitat, as we have lost our sense of courtesy and gratitude toward the land and its inhabitants. Our quests for progress and development, for power and control over nature have brought us to a wasteworld instead of a wonderworld. Our sole standard for success in agriculture has been production: land and farmers have been asked only to produce, and it has been assumed that competition and innovation would solve all problems. Agricultural practices for the past 50 years have ascribed almost no importance to the preservation of the land, to its fertility and ecological health; they have ignored or defied our natural knowledge of the Earth that sustains us.

People who use the land must know it well and must have the motivation and freedom to use it well. Food is of the Earth and we are of the Earth. The meaning of such a simple truth eludes the corporate mind that is concerned only with economic return. Nurturing the Earth is about nurturing ourselves.

CHAPTER ONE

The Nature of Organic Growing

C hemical-based food-growing practices have been pervasive in North America since the 1950s. The results? Pesticide use has increased tenfold, yet crop loss due to pests has doubled. Topsoil erosion, water degradation and food contamination have reached horrendous levels.

Chemical farming is now being seen for what it is: a quick-fix approach that looks good at first but has serious and dangerous consequences. It is the health and viability of the soil that is of paramount importance. Plants grown with chemical fertilizers will likely yield good food at first, given good soil to start with. But growing food year after year with only chemical boosters and biocides impoverishes the soil and results ultimately in striking deterioration in food quality. Likewise, soil that is poor to start with won't grow abundant, high-quality food with organic methods until the land has been well-managed for some years.

The organic movement is finally coming of age. People want to eat food that is as safe and nutritious as the food served on farm tables in days gone by. Well-managed farms growing diverse crops without chemicals are proving more productive and more profitable than those using chemicals. The organic industry has been growing at the rate of 30 percent a year and the demand for organic food is currently much greater than the supply. Farmers and gardeners everywhere are responding to this demand, taking a giant step back to the future and turning to sustainability by switching to organic techniques.

Reversing Past Practices

Certainly the first step in going organic is to stop using chemical weed killers and bug killers. Nearly 500 insects, 230 crop diseases and 220 weeds have now developed immunity to biocides. Pesticides, herbicides and fungicides are a hazard to us and our environment and cause more problems than they attempt to solve. The desire to create a cosmetically perfect landscape has inadvertently turned many of our backyards into toxic sites that are inhospitable to wildlife, pets and children, not to mention ourselves.

The second step is to stop using synthetic fertilizers. It is generally known that they do not benefit the soil, but the harm that they do is only now being widely recognized. Chemical fertilizers dissolve quickly in water, rapidly increasing the levels of nitrate, phosphate and potassium available to plants. This is the seemingly desired effect. As they do this, however, they impede the activity of soil organisms that make nitrogen and phosphorus more gradually available to plants over time and they inhibit the absorption of the elements calcium and magnesium, which are essential to plant health. The net result is soft, abundant top growth and reduced soil fertility. The lush growth looks more appetizing and indeed it is — to a host of pests. As well, the imbalance of growth makes plants more disease-prone. Soils also become more acidic with the addition of synthetic fertilizers. This acidity repels beneficial earthworms and changes soil structure by dissolving the material that cements soil particles together. Rivers and lakes also become more acidic as soluble fertilizers leach into them.

And now there is a very new practice, the genetic manipulation of plants, that also must be reversed before it is too late. Genetic engineering is the latest rung on the chemical-farming ladder. The biotechnology industry, in multimillion-dollar publicity campaigns, promises to feed the world by splicing together alien genes to produce superfoods that contain their own pesticides and herbicide resistance.

But that technology is fraught with unknown risks and unanswered questions; it derives from the same desire to control and commodify nature by putting plants on a speed trip and killing anything that gets in the way. The third step in going organic is to not use seeds that have been genetically modified or products that have been derived from genetically altered seeds.

The Basics of Organic Growing

Organic gardening has often been defined as "growing without the use of chemical pesticides and artificial fertilizers." This is only a partial description, however, and implies that organic growers leave their gardens and fields to nature. Rather, organic growers use many techniques in order to work as closely as possible with nature. The main aim is to create a healthy, balanced environment and to renounce the mode of thinking wherein every insect is a pest, every uncultivated plant a weed and the solution to every problem a spray.

Organic growing is a process of attunement that calls for looking at and responding to the whole ecosystem in which plants are growing, rather than concentrating on isolated aspects. Modern science has confirmed what non-technological societies have always known: that the vitality of any system is maintained by the interaction of all its parts.

Organic gardeners employ a wide range of methods and materials aimed at soil care. In fact, their central maxim is "feed the soil." Soil is the ongoing result or function of a whole living environment, not simply the stuff that keeps the plants upright. Organic soil additions aim to feed the entire spectrum of soil life, from worms to microscopic bacteria whose activities release food for plants gradually, in balanced form.

A fertile soil not only contains such plant foods in appropriate sufficiency but also has a compositional structure that provides the living conditions suitable to both soil organisms and plant roots. To maintain the structure and fertility of the soil, organic growers grow cover crops and green manures and apply animal manures, mulches, seaweed and compost. These strategies all require knowledge and expertise and go hand in hand with soil-testing and cultivation practices for maximum soil benefit. For example, tractors and tillers are not operated when they might unnecessarily compact the soil.

On the other hand, there are organic products designed specifically to feed plants rather than the soil. Kelp meal, fish meal and rock phosphate are common organic fertilizers. They differ from artificial fertilizers in that they need to break down in the soil before they become available to plants.

The main thrust of pest and disease management for organic growers is to create the healthy soil and balanced environment that will produce strong, vigorous plant growth and deter outbreaks of pests and diseases in the first place. They also plant a wide range of crops so that disease or insect damage to one variety is not calamitous. But organic practitioners also employ direct strategies to maintain healthy plants. They pick off bugs and remove diseased plant parts by hand. They use mechanical protections, such as barriers around brassica plants to ward off the cabbage root fly, mini-greenhouses (sometimes called cloches) to keep slugs and snails away from young plants, and timely sowings to take advantage of insect cycles. Biological controls for pests, such as parasitic wasps, predatory mites, *Trichoderma* fungus and *Bacillus thuringensis*, cause minimal harm to the environment. Because rhubarb and garlic generally repel bugs, sprays made from these plants usually help protect more vulnerable plants.

In nature there are rarely great pest and disease problems; every creature has its place and is kept there by the interplay of other species. The more diverse a garden the more likely it is to attract the wide range of organisms that will maintain a dynamic balance by their own nature. The organic gardener often encourages natural controls by providing a large range of habitats and food plants in the garden. This may be done by providing nesting sites to attract birds, planting native trees, shrubs and hedges, leaving patches of long grass or weedy areas as protective covers, growing specific plants to attract beneficial insects or making a small pond as a home for frogs and toads. Identifying a pest or disease and learning about its habits and life cycle are fascinating avocations that both help the gardener decide whether the problem really merits action and prevent the killing of beneficial insects and plants.

The organic grower's aim is not the eradication of any species, but a willingness to live in harmony with the fluctuating balance that is inherent in any life system. The organic philosophy respects the life-giving properties of food rather than the dubious aesthetics of perfection. Occasional bites or blemishes on fruit, leaf or root don't cause the organic gardener to throw arms up in despair and toss away the food as unacceptable.

The organic grower prefers to keep weeds under control rather than eliminate them entirely. There are no organic weed killers, but there are a variety of control methods beyond hoeing, hand weeding and rototilling. Thick, light-excluding mulches will suppress and eventually kill the majority of weeds. Green manures inhibit weed growth as well. Vegetables grown in blocks at close spacing will need far less weeding than those in conventional rows. Another technique is to let the first flush of weeds appear in a prepared bed and clean it before sowing the intended crop.

The organic approach to growing food demands a little more time and work than the quick-fix one whereby long-range costs are ignored. The organic gardener considers this exercise and reflection to be joyful and dignified activities that bring greater understanding of and respect for natural processes. Underlying the organic approach is the belief that we are not separate from the food we eat, nor from the soil in which it grows. Soil is not something to be owned and mined. We belong to it as much as earthworms or bean plants do. In truth, we borrow our lives from it.

Organic *and* Sustainable

"Sustainable" is often a word used to help define "organic" — usually in the context of growing practices that are intended to achieve "sustainable" productivity.

The concept of sustainability implies more than safe food-growing practices that maximize the soil's inherent fertility. Sustainable growing does not exhaust the resources of any given place and moves toward independence from those external inputs that require reliance on someone else's system.

Corn, for example, is a heavy feeder that can present a dilemma for the grower aiming for sustainability. It is difficult to maintain soil fertility in corn patches using only traditional organic methods, such as composting and cover cropping. Growing lots of corn year after year usually means dependence on relatively high levels of fertilizer from outside the garden. Having to obtain fertilizer, even if it is "organic," could represent either a sustainable or a non-sustainable practice. Buying manure from cattle feedlots, for example, carries a greater environmental debt than would getting it from your neighbour. Seaweed may be available from a nearby harbour, but excessive gathering can destroy a fragile ecosystem. Bonemeal, bloodmeal and cottonseed meal may sound like wonderful fertilizers. However, as their names imply, bonemeal and bloodmeal generally come from animals, some of which are diseased; most are raised in conditions that are ecologically destructive. Cottonseed meal comes from the cotton plant, the most pesticide-ridden crop in North America.

On a broader scale, there are few organic farmers or gardeners who are ready to relinquish dependence on petrochemicals to power machinery and to deliver goods and services. Yet it is possible to make choices that lessen reliance on non-renewable resources. A rototiller can be a more appropriate tool than a tractor and a walking hand cultivator can often serve better than a rototiller. A locally produced soil amendment may be the best "buy" when the fact that it didn't have to be transported thousands of kilometres to your garden is taken into account.

The organic movement has embraced the concept of sustainability in recent years. The term "sustainable gardening" marries organic growing methods and places them in a context of interpersonal commitment and global responsibility. Organic, sustainable gardening goes beyond the insular notion of a home garden to a vision that values all living communities or ecosystems on the planet, the health of each fostering the health of all.

This book does not focus on the tools and products that maintain the grower's status as consumer, but rather on the attitudes, techniques and the foods themselves that make for good growing and good eating. The next two chapters present an overview of traditional organic soil enhancement methods. I hope they offer helpful hints to old gardeners as well as new, and give a sense of organics to you who want to enjoy but not necessarily grow organic food.

CHAPTER TWO

Composting

M aking your own compost is a magical act. You bring together mouldy bread, apple cores, grass clippings, salad trimmings, leaves, straw, eggshells and wood ashes and it all becomes rich, dark brown, sweet-smelling earth. You add fresh compost to your garden beds and the plants that grow there are free of disease and pests, as well as being the most vibrant you've ever seen.

What Is Compost?

You'll find the spongy and moist, dark brown or black substance called humus on any forest floor. When plants and creatures die, they are consumed by billions of soil organisms and reduced to their elemental ingredients with no hint of their original form. Humus is the lifeblood of productive soil. It makes the difference between eroded, burned-out wasteland and flourishing forest, farm, garden or orchard where varied biological systems thrive in balance.

The only difference between a gardener's finished compost and humus found in the forest is the time it takes to produce them — on the average, three to six months for compost and 500 to 1,000 years for a couple of centimetres of forest topsoil.

Here's how it works. When appropriate materials are gathered together in a loose heap, microorganisms such as bacteria, fungi, actinomycetes and algae start to feed on the softer, more succulent parts. Their numbers increase rapidly, as does the rate of decomposition. (A mere gram of humus-rich soil contains several billion bacteria, about a million fungi, 10 million to 20 million actinomycetes and up to a million algae!) If the heap is large enough to build the heat all this activity produces, the temperature can reach 70°C (160°F), hot enough to deactivate weed seeds. Once the tender material is consumed, the compost pile cools and allows larger decomposers such as earthworms, beetles and centipedes to move in. (Earthworm castings are three times richer in nitrogen, twice as rich in exchangeable calcium, seven times richer in available phosphorus and 11 times richer in available potassium than the soil they process.) By the end of the decomposition, most of the original ingredients will have been broken down, mixed together and rebuilt into dark, rich-looking, crumbly compost. A carefully tended pile of well-prepared materials can be used as compost in just a few weeks.

The Process

You don't have to be a particularly knowledgeable or dedicated gardener to make your own compost. All the gardener or humus maker does is help speed along the natural process by which organic materials break down. The aim is to provide air, moisture and suitable food in the right proportions to keep the beneficial organisms functioning as desired. Most compost materials are either kitchen wastes or garden debris. Composting success depends on mixing the right combination of materials, allowing air to get at the compost and keeping the pile moist but not soggy. If there is too much moisture and insufficient air, different organisms take over and anaerobic (without oxygen) decomposition takes place — a process that is slower, smellier and doesn't produce much heat. If materials are too dry, decomposition will be very slow. However, compost piles are very forgiving: whatever your style or method, they always reward your efforts.

What to Use

The type of organic waste you use to build your compost heap is largely determined by available materials. Most kitchen wastes and leftovers, whether raw or cooked, are ideal. Meat and bones, however, are likely to attract rats and other animals, and fats, grease and oils are as hard for microbes to digest as they are for humans. Animal manures from farm animals make excellent additions to compost. You can add seaweed, algae, sods, sawdust (preferably weathered), eggshells, coffee grounds, straw, hay, weeds, wood ashes, pulverized nuts and seashells, as well as chopped plant stalks and leaves. The smaller the compost materials, the faster the composting process. The more kinds of ingredients, the better. Green matter has abundant moisture and nitrogen and breaks down rapidly, but a pile made mostly from grass clippings or leaves may become very soggy. Absorbent but dry, weathered material balances fresh vegetable or garden matter and provides better ventilation.

It is usually easiest and most efficient to build a compost pile in more or less equal layers, alternating dry materials that are high in carbon, such as straw, sawdust and corn stalks, with green, high-nitrogen materials, such as grass clippings, manure and vegetable trimmings. A good rule of thumb is to avoid layers more than 15 centimetres (six inches) thick of any one material.

Tips for Success

There are myriad ways to build a compost pile. I usually begin by choosing a sunny, airy, accessible location away from standing water. Then I loosen the soil to a depth of 30 centimetres (one foot) or more to provide good drainage and expose the bottom layer to soil organisms. Next I lay down about 15 centimetres (six inches) of roughage to ensure a good flow of air into the pile. Plant stalks, miscellaneous brush cuttings and prunings can be used. I then put down a layer of dry matter such as straw, leaves, old garden waste or hay and on top of that a few centimetres of green vegetation and kitchen waste. (I frequently use leaves from my nearby comfrey patch, and kitchen wastes fill a bucket under our kitchen sink every three or four days.) I lightly cover these first layers with soil and/or wood ashes to prevent odours and avoid attracting flies. The pile is built to shoulder height by adding new layers of dry vegetation, green vegetation, kitchen waste and soil as these materials become available.

A minimum volume of .09 cubic metres (three cubic feet) — .1 cubic metres (four cubic feet) in cold climates — is needed to properly insulate the heat of the composting process, but in the end it will shrink to less than half this mass. I water the pile whenever necessary to keep everything wet but not soggy. ("Soggy" means being able to squeeze water from a handful.) In wet weather, I sometimes cover the pile with burlap to keep it from becoming too moist.

Using my favourite digging fork, I turn the mixture every week or two and bring the outer parts to the centre. I try to maintain an adjacent open space to facilitate this task. If the sizes of the particles I've added are small and the weather warm, and if I turn my pile every few days, I get good compost in about three weeks. More often my compost piles are ready in two to six months.

Rather than let finished compost deteriorate I add it to the garden, spreading it 2.5 centimetres (one inch) or more thick on beds and around plantings or mixing it into the soil with my fork. I also screen it to use in potting mixes or to provide an especially fine soil surface. Mature compost smells good, crumbles in your hands and has few discernible remains of original ingredients.

More Helpful Hints

Composting in the above manner takes approximately equal amounts by weight of dry vegetation, fresh wastes and soil. A lot of composting recipes recommend natural "activators" to help start and maintain fermentation in the heap. These include alfalfa meal, animal manures and matured compost. I add thin layers of these if available, but I find that ordinary soil contains an adequate starter supply of microorganisms. I also favour comfrey and nettle leaves to help get the bacterial bonfire going.

Some composters add material as available and some collect material beside the compost site until there is enough to make a .09- or .1-cubic-metre (three- or four-cubic-foot) heap all at once. Some composters don't turn their pile, some turn it once with a fork, some turn it often with a shovel. (Turning a pile is great exercise or hard work, depending on who is doing it!) To increase aeration and speed decomposition, some composters stand perforated pipes in the middle as they're building their compost; others plunge composting wands, pipes or wooden stakes through the completed pile, then wiggle and jiggle them.

A compost pile needn't be contained, but usually it is neater, more efficient and manageable to enclose the operation. Again, whatever works is fine and at most anything works.

Many gardening centres sell a variety of composting units. For those with the time and energy to make their own, possibilities abound. On the smallest scale, a barrel, wooden box or large garbage can with the lid removed and holes in the sides might serve to begin composting. Homemade holding bins can be wood-and-wire units, four wooden pallets nailed together, or a circular standing wire mesh unit. These "holding" apparatus, however, do not allow easy turning of the materials. Bins that permit rotation of the compost are more efficient and can easily be constructed out of cinder blocks, wood, bricks or chicken wire. Fast compost is often made in a series of large bins with accessible sides that open for emptying. A fresh pile is built in the first unit, then mixed and turned into the second when the temperature of the pile falls; undigested material is moved to the centre of this second heap. A few weeks later the completed pile is turned into a third bin, ready to be used in the garden.

The Benefits

A compost program sustains garden soil in maximum health with little or no expense. It is almost impossible to overuse compost: the more you dig into your soil, the better. Compost improves the texture and structure of all soils, turning stodgy clay into friable loam and loose sand into retentive earth. The microbes that feed on soil humus continuously excrete a whole range of organic compounds. These bind soil particles together in a manner that ensures good aeration, drainage and water retention plus resistance to erosion. Even a small amount of compost spread over a garden has a beneficial inoculant effect on the soil due to the rapidity with which microorganisms multiply.

Compost acts as a storehouse and natural timed-release dispenser of plant nutrients. Microorganisms in humus bind chemical elements and release them gradually as the plants need them. Synthetic chemicals aren't as versatile: once dissolved in the soil water, they are taken up by the plant roots only in whatever combination they were added.

Compost harbours earthworms and beneficial fungi that fight nematodes and other soil pests. Recent studies have shown that plants grown in organically composted soil take up less lead and other pollutants. Compost contributes a high volume of top-quality organic matter to the soil without tying up garden space (as cover crops do) and it stabilizes soil pH at a neutral to slightly acid level — the ideal range for most vegetables. (The pH scale runs from 0, which is pure acid, to 14, which is pure lye. From the neutral point, 7, the numbers increase or decrease in geometric progression: thus, pH 5 is 10 times more acidic than pH 6, pH 4 is 100 times more acidic, et cetera.)

Composting is also an ecologically responsible activity. No matter what composting procedures one follows, precious resources are conserved rather than squandered in already overflowing garbage landfills. Careless agriculture and silviculture practices have depleted our life-supporting topsoil to the extent that we have already lost over 75 percent of this most precious resource. It can take 500 years for nature to build 2.5 centimetres (one inch) of topsoil, yet North American land is currently losing this much every 16 years. With less than 15 centimetres (six inches) of topsoil remaining, catastrophe is imminent.

About one-third of our household garbage consists of organic materials that can be recycled back into the ground. People who don't have gardens can save compostable materials for friends and neighbours who do. Dedicated composters can approach stores and restaurants, local sawmills and park commissions and boards for vast amounts of organic refuse that can be returned to the soil. Even at the home-garden level, composting makes a strong contribution to regenerating and replenishing the soil.

Our throwaway mentality has come from an exaggerated sense of our own power over nature. Composting consciousness reveres the myriad life forms of the soil, bows low in the alchemical dance of earth, air, fire and water, and humbly yet proudly co-creates bounteous riches for life to come. The shepherding of compostable material means we shall not want. Composting is the ultimate in recycling: the land provides our food, clothing and shelter and we close the circle by intensifying the fertility and health of the earth.

CHAPTER THREE

Cover Cropping and Mulching

As with composting, the desirability of cover cropping and mulching stems from the fundamental organic principle of feeding the soil rather than the plant.

Most cover crops are grains or legumes grown primarily to be mixed directly back into the soil or to be cut down and composted. Cover cropping has been an agricultural tradition for centuries and home gardeners are now starting to realize its benefits. Mulching, on the other hand, is familiar to many gardeners. It involves placing materials on top of the soil where plants are or will be growing.

Either technique can be used in small or large areas, throughout or in part of a garden or farm. They cost very little, yet reap enormous benefits. Both techniques feed the soil naturally with organic matter crucial for vital, healthy, productive growing. They protect the surface layer of the soil, increasing the beneficial activity of bacteria, fungi and earthworms. At the same time they prevent soil from washing or blowing away, baking dry, or compacting under heavy rain. Cover crops and mulches do an excellent job of suppressing weeds as well.

COVER CROPS

Specific Benefits

- Cover crops, also known as green manures, have the potential to supply most of a garden's nutritional needs.
- They condition both clay and sandy soils, moderating either extreme. Legumes especially will loosen compaction and add humus in heavy clay soils.
- Leguminous cover crops — clovers, alfalfa, vetches, peas and beans — can also provide a bonus of extra nitrogen in soil by "fixing" it from the air and storing it in nodules along their roots.
- In sandy soils, the bulky, deep roots of cereal crops draw up needed phosphorus, potassium and trace minerals that would otherwise be below the reach of most vegetable roots.
- The matted roots of cereal crops enable the soil to absorb more water. They keep plant foods locked up in their tissues until decay releases them for a succeeding crop.

Disadvantages

- In a large space, turning over a green manure by hand is very labour-intensive. (But a rototiller works wonders.)
- Cover crops can take up space during the growing season that could be producing lots of food.

Common Cover Crops

Legumes

- Alfalfa is hard to establish unless your soil is well-drained and fairly neutral. It has deep taproots and is a very productive nitrogen-fixer. Alfalfa can be cut several times annually for mulch. A stand of alfalfa can last many years if not turned over.
- Clovers tolerate humid and acidic conditions much more than alfalfa. Dutch White clover is low-growing and great as a living mulch. The biennial clover Alsike is the most tolerant of wet and acidic soils. Other clovers include Red, Sweet White and White Ladino, which prefer loamy soil, plus Crimson and Sweet Yellow, which are more adaptable.
- Fava beans are widely adaptable, have low fertility needs, tolerate acidic soils and fix high amounts of nitrogen. They thrive under cool growing conditions and will normally survive a coastal winter if fall-planted. When planted in the spring, they can produce a high-protein summer crop. As with other legumes, their roots can be left in the ground at harvest time and the foliage can either be composted or mulched down on the spot and covered with hay, leaves or other mulch material.
- Soybeans and other warm-weather beans are ideally planted in May or June to serve as both a food and cover crop.
- The vetches tolerate a wide range of soils and have both low fertility needs and high drought tolerance. Hairy vetch is the hardiest and is often overwintered with oats and rye. It prefers a well-drained soil.

- Field peas fix the least nitrogen of the legumes. Austrian Winter pea thrives in cool, moist conditions, so is a popular winter cover crop on the West Coast. It is a good weed competitor, especially when sown with oats.
- Lupines have deep roots and make a dependable first crop in a rebuilding scheme. Large White lupine is the most winter-hardy.
- Chick-peas or garbanzo beans are among the highest nitrogen-fixers and are also a nutritious and delicious food.
- Phacelia, a still-underappreciated annual, is an excellent nitrogen-fixer as well as being a very ornamental plant that bees love.

Grains
- Winter rye tops the list of the best, non-legume winter cover crops. The seeds germinate in cool fall weather, the plants tolerate extremely cold temperatures and they resume growing in the spring to prevent topsoil erosion from heavy spring rains.
- Barley prefers a neutral to alkaline pH and is highly drought-tolerant. It can be sown in fall or spring and turned under in spring or fall.
- Buckwheat is an excellent soil-builder. With an early start, gardeners can turn under two or three crops a season, adding great amounts of organic matter to the soil. Buckwheat draws up phosphorus from deeper soil levels and is high in calcium. It will grow in poor soil and is miraculous at suppressing weeds. Its white flowers are much sought-after by bees and it readily reseeds itself if not turned under. It will not tolerate frost, so should be planted from late spring onward.

- Millet tolerates poor and dry acidic soils and should be sown in spring to be turned under in the fall.
- Oats can be grown in a variety of soils but do best in cool, moist conditions. As a green manure planted in spring, it grows well with peas and beans. For a winter cover, oats should be planted early in fall since it dies after the first hard frost.
- Annual ryegrass also dies in winter, so it should be planted by late August to leave a thatch of stubby residue through till spring. Both ryegrass and oats allow crops to be planted earlier in spring than winter rye, but they contribute less organic matter and are less of a deterrent to spring weeds.
- Spring wheat is sown in the spring to be turned under in the fall and winter wheat is sown in the fall to be turned under in the spring. Both prefer a fertile, loamy, not-too-acidic soil, but both tolerate low-moisture conditions.

Rye and wheat both contain natural toxins that will suppress not only weed growth but also insect pests in subsequent crops.

Further Considerations

After turning under a green manure, delay planting for at least a week in the case of legumes and two weeks for grains. Early decomposition gives off ethylene gas that inhibits seed germination; also, multiplying microorganisms temporarily use up available nitrogen as they break down the green manure. Winter rye and winter barley release toxins that can affect emerging veggies as well as weed seedlings. How long it takes the cover crop to decay sufficiently is directly related to how fibrous and mature it is when turned under. Most green manures are incorporated into the soil while they are still lush and green and therefore break down fairly fast. If they mature past this stage, plants start to consist of much more carbon than nitrogen. In this case, the addition of composted manure or other nitrogen sources can speed the decomposition process, as can a dusting of lime if your soil is on the acidic side.

Most common cover crops are available through garden centres. Merchants will also provide information on seeding rates, depths to cover seed, best varieties for your garden, best times to turn crops and whatever other questions you may have.

Cover cropping is a very open-ended concept. My own cover crops are all the pea, bean and grain varieties described in the next section of this book. As a rule, I eat or sell only seeds of the current year; older seeds get recycled back into the garden, where they may become simply green manures or double again as cover crops, food or seed.

Even if you have space available for only two months, it's amazing how quickly cover crops such as buckwheat and oats can grow. In certain places, even weeds can be allowed lush growth before turning them under if you're careful about not letting the most pernicious ones go to seed. In fact, the possibility of utilizing weeds as a green manure (or in the compost pile or as mulch) reflects the organic philosophy that proper management techniques can enliven the biological relevance of everything in the garden.

COMPLEMENTARY TECHNIQUES

Crop rotation and intercropping are refinements of cover cropping that involve only a little more planning. Many cultures have relied successfully on these techniques to maintain soil fertility. They can be used with much benefit in small gardens or large farms.

Crop Rotation

Crop rotation is the practice of alternating both cover crops and food plants on the same piece of ground. Developing a rotation scheme can extend the advantages of green manuring in many ways. Rotations further improve soil structure and increase soil nitrogen, bacterial activity and the release of carbon dioxide. They help keep pests in balance and discourage certain weeds from gaining a foothold, especially when repeated over several years. A sequence that includes deep-rooted food followed by a cover crop extracts nutrients from layers of the soil not used by shallow rooters, leaves pathways for the roots of less vigorous crops, and increases the depth of the topsoil.

There are many beneficial ways to rotate crops. A general principle is to avoid planting successive crops that are related botanically, that have common diseases or pests, or have the same soil requirements. This requires experience and/or a little homework, but is well worth the effort.

Rotations can be sequential or overlapping. In either case, however, it helps to know what nutrients each crop takes from the soil as well as the fertilization and cultivation methods to which each responds. For instance, sweet corn, in contrast to most other crops, does well following any member of the Brassica family. To take advantage of this you could, for example, sow a leguminous green manure under established cabbage, let it overlap the cabbage harvest, then turn it under the following spring to provide good growing conditions for sweet corn.

Because of the pervasiveness of monoculture farming, where the same crop is grown in the same place year after year, research in crop rotation is scanty. Some studies have been done, however, on how crop rotation affects yields. They show that any given crop can affect the succeeding one or be affected by the preceding one. For instance, onions, lettuces, squash and legumes help succeeding crops, but onions themselves are not benefited by a preceding legume. Potatoes yield highest after corn. Soybeans greatly decrease the incidence of scab in succeeding potato crops, whereas peas, oats and barley increase it. Carrots, beets and cabbage often reduce the yield in crops that follow them, but corn and beans are not affected negatively by the preceding crop.

Rotation schemes also take into account crop preferences for the timing of soil amendments, such as compost and animal manures. For instance, cabbages, tomatoes and root crops grow better on ground manured the previous year, while corn and squash do well in ground manured the same year.

Basically crop rotation means variety, which gives stability to biological systems. The longer the rotation period before the same crop is grown again, the better. Many organic farmers practise five-year or even eight-year rotations, but shorter rotations can be valuable in small-scale gardens. Planning is necessary, as many factors need to be taken into account in setting up the sequences. One example you might try is a two-year rotation: peas, then beans, then a grain during the first year, followed in year two by a heavy feeder such as corn, and then another planting of grain. In each case all residues are returned to the soil. Another possibility is to have two simultaneous gardens — one for vegetables and one for green manures — in which plots are rotated yearly.

The rotation of crops with grazing pastures for animals grown for food requires greater planning skills on the part of the organic grower. The provision of your own animal manures in conjunction with green manures facilitates more efficient and sustainable management of soil fertility. The best book I've seen on maintaining organic livestock is the *Organic Livestock Handbook*, put out by Canadian Organic Growers and edited by Anne Macey (Box 6408, Station J, Ottawa, Ont. K2A 3Y6).

Intercropping

Intercropping refers to growing two or more crops together for greater productivity and more efficient use of resources. This practice is also referred to as undersowing or as a particular type of companion planting: the latter usually involves food crops intended for harvest, whereas undersowing most often indicates a leguminous green manure grown along with a food crop. White clover has been found to have the best prospects as an undersown cover crop that enriches the soil with nitrogen while not impeding the growth of most food crops.

Many gardeners are familiar with the native North American tradition of companion-planting corn, beans and squash — the beans growing up the corn and providing nitrogen, while the squash suppresses weeds. I sometimes plant winter cauliflower in the shade of corn or maturing fava beans. Russian winter kale is a very hardy and delicious winter green that often keeps my winter barley company, though I sow it much earlier for abundant winter picking.

MULCHING

Specific Benefits

Like cover cropping, mulching protects and enriches the soil and suppresses weeds admirably. Mulch materials are usually placed around growing plants or on ground where plants are soon to be. Thus mulch has more immediate benefits than green manures.

- Mulch prevents crusting of the soil surface and creates ideal seeding conditions at the interface of soil and mulch. It retains moisture and keeps the soil surface damp. This reduces the need to water, as well as the amount of water required, and allows the garden to be safely left for longer periods of time.
- It results in a light and fluffy, porous soil that enhances root development and effective drainage.
- It keeps soil cooler in summer and warmer in fall and winter, prolonging the harvest of such crops as lettuce and peas and reducing the dangers of freezing and ground heaving.

- It supports weak or top-heavy plants and keeps sprawling vegetables mud-free and dry, preventing mildew, mould, rust and blight.
- It's effective in decreasing wind and water erosion from the sloping sides of raised beds.
- It saves a lot of time and energy (and backs) in the long run. It can eliminate most digging and all of the traditional "turning of the garden" in spring. This avoids disturbing the soil layers and preserves intricate earthworm tunnels. It also eliminates the need for most hoeing and weeding; weeds that do poke through after repeated mulching are weakly rooted and easy to pull, or may be mulched over yet again.
- A thick layer of mulch prolongs root-crop storage in the garden, right where the vegetables grew.
- Plastic mulches, though not my choice for both aesthetic and environmental reasons, can help the earth absorb and retain heat, resulting in more vigorous growth.

Ruth Stout's Permanent Mulch System involves a year-round covering of the garden surface with continuously added layers of organic material. In this system, mulching becomes the main or ongoing garden task and eliminates most of the weeding, hoeing and digging. This gardener, however, always stops short of such a total mulching scheme because of the pleasure and satisfaction I get from those very activities.

Disadvantages
Some hot-weather crops may be slowed down somewhat by cooler soil under mulch.

Avoid mulching if success with melons, squash, cukes and tomatoes is already chancy, or delay using mulch until the weather is hot.

Seedlings planted in very moist soil and mulched immediately can succumb to the soil borne fungal disease called damping-off, which can eat through young stems in a matter of hours.

Mulching on heavy, waterlogged soils can rot the crown and main roots of certain plants such as rhubarb. Again, mulching can be postponed until the soil is drier. Absorbent mulches already in place should be pulled back from the base of the plants to allow the soil to dry and ventilate.

Mulching promotes and harbours slugs. The list of recommended slug control methods includes snakes, toads, ducks, geese, chickens, traps, lures, barriers, beer, salt, sprays and wood ashes and I've got the first four of these! Slugs dislike sharp, bristly edges, so fluffing up straw or hay mulch rather than matting it down can be quite effective.

Common Mulches

- Straw, which is essentially the bare stalks left after the grain heads have been harvested, is one of the best all-round mulches, being lightweight, attractive and easy to handle.
- Hay as a mulch usually contains weed seeds — probably no problem in garden paths, but definitely not the mulch to use in a bed of spring bulbs or in the onion patch.
- Leaves are widely available, easy to handle and excellent sources of humus when they break down into the soil.

- Wood chips, wood shavings and shredded bark are best used for mulching garden paths. But don't take them from mills where they might be contaminated. Woodchips and bark are usually applied several centimetres deep over a few layers of newspaper. They are not recommended as mulch for vegetables, because they deplete soil nitrogen and take up to three years to decompose.
- Sawdust, also when clean, is especially useful for spreading around small plants or along narrow footpaths. The best sawdust always comes from the bottom of the pile, so try for that.
- Grass clippings are easy to obtain in summer and handy to spread in small places. Because of their nitrogen content they heat up readily, so avoid placing them against sensitive plant roots or stems.
- Seaweed and lake weed, when available and unpolluted, make rich, soil-building mulches, but follow the precautions given for grass clippings. I haven't found it necessary to wash salt from seaweed when using it in the garden.
- Newspapers, when covered with a more visually pleasing mulch, are efficient in suppressing weeds but, except for those that have vegetable inks on non-bleached paper, will pollute your soil with lead and dioxins. Cardboard is unbleached and a more effective mulch material as well.
- Green manures can serve as living mulches that discourage weeds and enrich soil, but timely application is important.

Cover cropping and mulching obviously involve a little more understanding and involvement than repeated applications of chemical fertilizers and poisons. They are enjoying a vigorous renaissance as we become more conscious of how impoverished and toxic our gardens and food have become. Involving little financial investment, they act in a manner similar to composting by fostering earthworms, beneficial nematodes, bacteria and countless other organisms that enrich simple dirt and regenerate it into lush loam. They are basic and practical methods to create organically rich soil that teems with life.

WEATHER WATCHING

One of the most important skills and practices of organics is weather watching. The organic grower, unlike the chemical one, is constantly in tune with her or his plants and is there to respond to any situation. Monoculture farming, in its adherence to preformulated schedules of biocide and fertilizer applications, is becoming increasingly hard-pressed to respond to the unpredictable weather it has been instrumental in creating.

As record heat, cold, rainfall and drought conditions continue to become more prevalent all over the globe, a lot of crops are not going to make it. By planting a diversity of crops, by protecting the soil with cover crops and mulches and by attuning to changing conditions every day, the organic grower increasingly will be the successful grower.

ORGANICS IN THE MIDST OF GENETICALLY MODIFIED ORGANISMS

The use of genetically modified organisms in chemical agriculture greatly increases the challenge to maintain the organic integrity of food crops.

To reduce the risk of contamination from direct GMO inputs and from drift, the organic grower must recognize potential points of contamination. GMOs might come into the farm from the use of shared equipment or from the field environment itself. To be certified, the farmer must now provide documentation demonstrating that the areas of risk have been assessed and a protection plan is in place.

Knowledge of the land is crucial for protection against GMOs. It is necessary to know the patterns of prevailing wind and water runoff if neighbours uphill or upwind are growing GMO crops, and to know what buffers to employ. Cross-pollination by wind is a special concern in the case of corn and canola, and cross-pollination by bees can occur for distances of up to four kilometres (2.5 miles).

Genetically modified seeds are now appearing in seed catalogues, inoculants are now being genetically engineered to extend shelf life and transport equipment often contains residues of GMO products. Most organic certifiers now require growers to use certified organic seed. All of this necessitates more research and documentation on the part of the organic grower wanting to maintain certification and makes the certification process much more tedious. Organic certification inspectors are performing an increasingly difficult yet vitally important task.

Vigilance against GMOs also, of course, adds to the expense of being organic.

There is a blatant unfairness when agrichemical interests point to organic products being more expensive. In a brighter tomorrow, food-growing methods that foster safety and well-being will receive funding for research and development rather than the crazy way things happen now. That tomorrow is just around the corner and can be hastened by a willingness to pay a little bit more for organic food.

The Food We Grow and Eat

two

I've owned and operated Salt Spring Seeds since 1986. I'm happy to do most of the seeding, maintenance and harvesting of our crops with my family and with our apprentices. Seeds and catalogues go out to about 6,000 people and my growing areas have been about one hectare. The crops that I encourage other people to grow are the ones we use ourselves.

It has been a very interesting journey for me as a gardener, farmer and seedsperson. The biggest surprises along the way were the crops described in this section. One of my original intentions was to see how much of my own food I could grow. I quickly came to see that any grower aiming for self-sufficiency and not relying on meat, fish and dairy products would have to embrace beans and grains.

In the early 1970s, *Diet for a Small Planet*, the best-selling book by Frances Moore Lappé, had challenged many of the assumptions of my meat- and dairy-based diet, the prime one being the need for a large daily intake of protein of animal origin. Lappé asserted that we North Americans were eating much more protein than our bodies could effectively utilize and that the quality of animal food we consumed could be equalled and surpassed by whole grains and beans.

Lappé's theories made sense to me: I believed I would be eating more efficiently and improving my health by eating from lower on the food chain. However, although I did considerable experimentation with her recipes, something didn't quite work. Mostly, the meals I prepared were not very exciting. Certainly they didn't reach the gustatory height of a juicy steak or even a Swiss cheese sandwich. Combining beans, grains, seeds and nuts at that time did little to change my culturally conditioned belief that such foods were the subsistence fare of less fortunate people.

I started converting to plant foods as the mainstay of my diet when I began growing my own beans and grains. The reason I hadn't done so earlier became obvious. Most of the foods advocated by Lappé and available back then were of notably poor quality. They were (and, for the most part, still are) so neglected by our food-production and marketing systems that what we could buy was often years old and/or not suitable for human consumption. For example, the promise of soybeans' wonderful nutritive qualities (including a 40 percent protein content) was never satisfyingly delivered by those obtainable in stores: after 24 hours of soaking, many water changes and several of hours cooking, they were still indigestible and insipid-tasting at best. Now I've created my own recipes, from my own soybean cultivars, that need only 90 minutes' cooking after four hours' soaking and are both digestible and delectable.

This section describes many high-protein plant foods that offer much better quality than commonly believed. As these foods have become a more substantial part of my diet and as I've related more directly to people from other cultures, I've learned how unjustified my bias against these foods has been. The range and subtleties of taste and texture that I've discovered in beans and grains make my meals both satisfying and exciting. I am more and more appreciating that people worldwide have sustained themselves sumptuously on plant foods, rather than having merely subsisted.

It seems even wiser these days to rely less on dairy, fish and meat products. The past few years have seen the rise of mad cow disease, chicken flu, tainted meat and dwindling fish stocks. Few of us can avoid the perils of factory-farmed animal food through raising our own; having access to enough land to care for cows, goats, pigs, chickens or fish is a rare luxury.

Fruit and nuts are certainly choice foods and I gratefully cultivate them. Leaf, fruit and root vegetables are excellent fare and I appreciate every one I grow. But these on their own don't come close to keeping me going during the cold winter months.

Beans and grains offer a deeper quality of nourishment. Through personal experience, I've come to believe that these foods are the key to sustaining both us and the Earth simultaneously.

Beans and grains are standard fare of ancient and modern cultures in temperate climates around the globe. I think that we in North America lost sight of their goodness with the development of large-scale agriculture focused on food for profit. The food industry as it now exists would collapse if we adopted whole beans and grains as the core of our diet. Given that nonorganic packaged and processed foods almost certainly contain GMOs as well as residues of herbicides and pesticides, I've been simplifying my own kitchen by cutting them out. And I'm encouraging you to do the same.

Beans and grains are extremely easy to grow. They do well in a wide range of conditions and do not require as much care and attention as regular vegetables.

Beans and grains are proficient producers of high-quality, substantial food. They can be eaten as the whole foods they are, rather than being processed into less health-enhancing products.

Beans and grains, when homegrown or obtained relatively fresh from the farmer, are far tastier and more digestible than the old and tired fare found in grocery stores. In the world of beans and grains there is an awesome diversity of flavours, textures and colours waiting to be appreciated and savoured.

Countless gardeners and farmers before us have infused their own unique love of the land into the beans and grains that are now our heritage.

CHAPTER FOUR

Grains: Wheat, Barley and Oats

Perhaps the most surprising garden revelation to me has been that grains are fabulous garden crops. Given the zillions of hectares that big-time agriculture devotes to grains in North America, why would you think of growing wheat, barley or oats in your garden?

Even to grow a small patch of grain once can give you an intimacy and appreciation for one of our basic foods that will last forever. And, if you're seriously thinking about growing more of your own food, nothing can be easier or more rewarding than grains. They grow like the grass of your lawn—only you allow them to mature instead of mowing them down.

Most people in North America have forgotten or have never known that grains can be cooked as the whole foods they are. If you don't mill them or pearl them or roll them but just cook them, you get all of their goodness. We're somewhat used to doing this with the rice that we import, but not with our own grains. Wheat, barley and oats are good sources of fibre, niacin, thiamine, iron, phosphorus and calcium.

There is another virtually unknown way of eating whole grains. If you soak them overnight and then rinse them twice a day for two days, you get a raw food with a soft yet crunchy texture and a rich, sweet taste. These sprouted berries of grain are bursting with energy and can be used in many delectable ways.

Grains grown for food make excellent compost and mulch material. After harvesting the seed heads, the oat, wheat or barley straw can be cut down and recycled in other parts of the garden or on the same bed.

Grain varieties that are most appropriate for backyard growers are not easily obtained. As has been the case with soybeans, agribusiness has focused on varieties for processing rather than for eating whole. But cultivars for direct consumption have been selected and maintained by cultures around the world for thousands of years.

In a world of rapidly diminishing grain reserves, rapidly increasing population and rapidly increasing costs of processing and transporting food, it's high time we began to appreciate not only the food quality whole grains provide but the energy savings as well.

Grains come with the huge bonus of their hardiness. In much of North America this means they can be sown in the fall and overwintered. Thus they can be cover crops and food crops simultaneously. They prevent erosion and condition the soil at a time when you normally wouldn't think of growing anything.

Soil Preference

Grains grow well in ordinary garden soil. Some varieties tend to get quite top-heavy in rich soil and fall over ("lodge") in wind or rain. This can be quite inefficient for machine combining but is not a big deal for a gardener harvesting by hand. Still, I usually sow my grains in my least-fertile ground. The root growth of wheat, barley and oats makes them excellent conditioners for both clay and sandy soil.

Varieties

It is important to realize the difference between hulled and "hulless" varieties and to grow the hulless ones. Seeds of all cultivars are coated by hulls but some have a thin, easy-to-remove hull and so have been given the "hulless" designation. Hulless grains are easily cleaned by hand or foot rubbing. Most commercial cultivars of oats and barley have tight, hard hulls that need to be threshed by machines. Varieties of spelt as well as some of the old wheats also require mechanical processing, but most modern wheats have loose-fitting hulls.

Planting Time

Here on the West Coast of B.C., I sow some of my wheats, barleys and oats any time from late September to early November. They make it through very soggy times as well as nights that go down to -15°C (5°F). Reports from customers across Canada indicate these crops can stand weather a lot colder than we have here. If not fall-planted, I recommend sowing them as soon as the ground can be worked in the spring. Grains appreciate an extended cooler season for growing and don't produce well in spring planting where summer follows right on the heels of winter. My fall-sown grains outyield my spring-sown ones, even though they are ready to harvest only a couple of weeks earlier.

Sowing

I think it a good idea for first-time garden grain growers to seed in rows in prepared soil. This makes it easier to know what you've planted when other grasses start appearing. I walk my row seeder the desired length of row, setting the depth to a seed's length below the surface. Alternatively, you can plant your grains by hand, sowing them a few finger widths apart. You needn't worry about thinning. After multiplying your crop for a season and learning what to expect, you might opt for planting in wide rows or blocks the next time around.

Maintenance

Weeding isn't as crucial as it is for other garden crops. You'll probably want to pull out other grasses to avoid confusion when harvesting and I certainly wouldn't tell you to stop eliminating customary bothersome weeds. But grains are quite adept at colonizing areas once they get growing.

Watering is also less of a consideration than for other crops. Grains are normally grown at times when there is abundant soil moisture. They are ready for harvesting by the time it gets hot and dry in late June and July.

Harvesting

Harvest when the seed heads have totally dried. Your fingernail won't be able to dent a ripe grain kernel. With an early April sowing, my barleys are usually ready by late June or early July and my oat and wheat crops a few weeks later. My preferred methods of harvesting are either to snip the seed head with scissors or snap them with thumb and forefinger into a bucket alongside.

Threshing

All manner of small-scale threshing equipment has been invented in countries where small-scale grain growing is common. But until an inexpensive, efficient thresher appears on North American markets I'm content to use my feet. I've made a wooden box about 60 centimetres by 90 centimetres (two feet by three feet) and 30 centimetres (one foot) high, to the bottom of which I've screwed thin wooden slats for extra abrasion. I get into my threshing box with the harvested grain and remove the hulls by the simple process of rubbing the grains against the bottom of the box with my shoes. This same shuffle performed on a tarp on flat ground would serve almost as well. I then blow the chaff away with the blow-nozzle attachment on my air compressor. A hair dryer, fan or the wind work also, as do appropriate screens. Any leftover chaff will rise to the water surface prior to cooking grain.

Yield

A 15-metre (50-foot) row can easily yield 4.5 kilograms (10 pounds) of grain and wide row plantings can yield much more. Grains multiply themselves very rapidly. A small packet can end up being enough to sow a half hectare after two years.

Cooking

Whole grains take about one hour's simmering to be cooked. Prior soaking speeds the process somewhat and renders the seeds more digestible for people who require that. Even with longer cooking, their texture will seem quite chewy to people used to soft rice, pearled barley or rolled oats. A bowl of cooked wheat berries does not get eaten very quickly. Cooked whole grains may take some getting used to for those accustomed to soft foods. I find their chewiness a very positive attribute, providing more flavour and expanding meals to a less-hurried affair. Learning to savour the longer eating time for cooked whole grains has been a good experience for me, though I grew up gulping and gobbling my food.

Saving Seed

Grain cultivars don't cross, so saving seed for planting is simply a matter of not eating all the harvest.

Genetically Modified?

No genetically modified wheats, barleys or oats are yet in the marketplace.

Outlook

I think small-scale grain growing is going to really catch on as gardeners realize how easy it is to grow such high-quality food. Harvesting and threshing the seed are somewhat labour-intensive, but the rest takes almost no time at all. We grow grains on a huge scale in North America, but have somehow missed the possibilities inherent in growing them in gardens and eating them as whole foods.

As people discover and begin to desire the wonderful array of colours, tastes and textures in grains, large-scale farmers will be encouraged to diversify their crops. They will be able to ask more for whole grains than the few pennies a kilogram they now receive for processing grains.

grains

BASIC STOVE-TOP WHOLE GRAIN

SERVES 2–3

| 1 CUP | WHOLE WHEAT, BARLEY OR OATS | 250 ML |
| 2 1/2 CUPS | WATER | 625 ML |

Bring grain and water to boil in pot or saucepan, then simmer for one hour or until all liquid has been absorbed.

After removing my grain from the stove I usually let it stand, covered, for a few minutes, then add a titch of salt and fluff it with a wooden spoon or fork.

Cooked whole oat, barley or wheat berries are a satisfying meal with a little flax oil, butter, soy sauce or other seasoning. Their flavour is enhanced by parsley, chives, fennel, garlic, basil, anise, caraway, rosemary and thyme. They enrich soups, stews and salads.

Kamut is a wheat that is becoming increasingly available as a whole grain. Sometimes called Polish wheat, it is higher in protein, vitamins and minerals than regular wheat and has kernels that are twice the size. As a cooked whole food, it has a rich corn-like flavour.

Cracked whole grains are a pleasant alternative if you have a flour mill or food processor. Process the grains until there are no whole ones. Cooking cracked berries takes half the time of whole grain and creates a porridge-like consistency.

BERRY YUMMY PILAF

SERVES 4

1 CUP	BARLEY, OAT OR WHEAT BERRIES	250 ML
2 3/4 CUPS	WATER OR VEGETABLE STOCK	680 ML
2 TBSP	OIL	30 ML
1	ONION, SLICED	1
1	CELERY STALK, CHOPPED FINE	1
2 CUPS	MUSHROOMS, SLICED	500 ML
2	GARLIC CLOVES, CHOPPED FINE	2
1/4 TSP	THYME	1 ML
1 TBSP	SOY SAUCE	15 ML
	SALT TO TASTE	

Simmer the whole grain in the water or stock for one hour as per basic recipe. (The extra 1/4 cup liquid will ensure sufficient moisture when combining.) Sauté the onion and celery in oil for about five minutes. Add the mushrooms, garlic and thyme, then sauté until the onion and celery are transparent and the mushrooms are slightly soft. Add the cooked grain to the sauté or vice versa and gently sauté or simmer the pilaf for five to 10 more minutes until the liquid is absorbed and the flavours blended. Season with soy sauce and salt.

Variations: Other vegetables such as carrots, parsnips, peppers, zucchini or squash may be substituted. Vary sautéeing time as necessary.

Toasted pumpkin or sunflower seeds make a crunchy and zesty topping.

WHOLE GRAIN AND TOMATO SALAD

SERVES 6

1/2 CUP	WHOLE WHEAT, BARLEY OR OATS	125 ML
1 1/4 CUPS	WATER	310 ML
2 CUPS	CHOPPED TOMATOES	500 ML
1/2 CUP	CHOPPED RED ONION	125 ML
1/4 CUP	PACKED FRESH BASIL LEAVES, CHOPPED	60 ML
2 TBSP	OLIVE OR FLAX OIL	30 ML
1 TBSP	RED WINE VINEGAR	15 ML
1	GARLIC CLOVE, MINCED	1
	SALT AND PEPPER TO TASTE	

Simmer the grain in the water for one hour. Allow to cool. In a large bowl, toss together the wheat, tomatoes and onion. Blend the basil, oil, vinegar and garlic. Pour the dressing over the salad and toss.

Best served right after preparation.

GOURMET GINGER GRAIN SOUP

SERVES 4–5

1/2 CUP	DRY BARLEY AND/OR WHEAT BERRIES	125 ML
2 TBSP	COOKING OIL	30 ML
1	ONION, CHOPPED	1
1 INCH	KNOB OF FRESH GINGER, GRATED	3 CM
1	CARROT, DICED	1
1	PARSNIP, DICED	1
1	MEDIUM POTATO, DICED	1
3	MEDIUM TOMATOES, CHOPPED	3
5 CUPS	VEGETABLE STOCK OR WATER	1.25 L
	SALT AND PEPPER TO TASTE	
	FRESH PARSLEY, MINCED	

Sauté onion and ginger in oil for five minutes. Stir in carrot, parsnip and potato and sauté for five minutes more. Add the tomatoes and whole grain. Combine with the stock in the soup pot and simmer for at least one hour. Add the salt and pepper near the end. Garnish with minced parsley.

For a more full-bodied soup, add a half cup of soup peas with the grain.

WHOLE GRAIN WITH PEAS

SERVES 4

1 CUP	FRESH OR FROZEN PEAS	250 mL
2 TBSP	FINELY CHOPPED SCALLION,	30 mL
	GARLIC GREENS OR CHIVES	
1 TBSP	OIL OR BUTTER	15 mL
2 CUPS	COOKED WHOLE WHEAT, BARLEY OR OATS	500 mL
1/2 TSP	SALT	2 mL

Stir peas, scallions and oil into the cooking grain just before it is done. Cover and simmer for five more minutes or until the peas are heated through. Add salt to taste.

Corn kernels work just as well as peas.

SPROUTED WHEAT SALAD

SERVES 4–5

2 CUPS	SPROUTED WHEATBERRIES (SEE BELOW)	500 mL
1	CUCUMBER, PEELED AND DICED	1
1	SWEET PEPPER, DICED	1
1	TOMATO, DICED	1
1	SCALLION, CHOPPED	1
1	SMALL CELERY STALK, DICED	1
2 TBSP	CHOPPED FRESH PARSLEY	15 mL
1/2 CUP	SALAD OIL	125 mL
1/2 CUP	FRESH LEMON JUICE	125 mL
	SALT TO TASTE	

Combine all ingredients in a large bowl. Toss to mix. Cover and refrigerate overnight before serving.

To sprout wheat berries, soak overnight in twice their volume of water. Drain. Rinse and drain two or three times a day for about three days until the sprouts are about one centimetre (one half inch) long.

BARLEY, LEEK AND LENTIL LIFT

SERVES 4–6

3 CUPS	FINELY CHOPPED LEEKS	750 mL
2 TBSP	OIL	30 mL
2 3/4 CUPS	STOCK OR WATER	680 mL
3/4 CUP	DRIED LENTILS	180 mL
1/2 CUP	BARLEY	125 mL
1	BAY LEAF	1
1/2 TSP	DRIED ROSEMARY	2 mL
	SALT AND SOY SAUCE TO TASTE	

Sauté leeks in oil in a large saucepan on medium-high heat until softened. Add stock and bring to a boil. Stir in lentils, barley, bay leaf and rosemary. Cover and simmer for 50 minutes or until liquid has been absorbed. Remove bay leaf. Season.

CHAPTER FIVE

Beans: Regular Old Chilies and Pintos

The beans I refer to in this chapter are the more common soup, pinto, chili, baking, salad and refry beans. Soybeans, adzukis, limas and tepary beans need the weather a little hotter than these, while favas, lentils and chick-peas prefer it a little cooler. Most of my comments, though, are relevant to all these beans, the myriad colours, shapes and sizes of which are still thrilling to me after 20 years of growing them.

Salt Spring Island, where I do my growing, is situated in British Columbia's Strait of Georgia between Vancouver and Victoria at 49°N and 123°W. Salt Spring doesn't get the concentrated summer heat familiar to most continental growers. Summer days rarely go above 27°C (80°F). Annual rainfall is about one metre (39 inches), most of which falls between October and April. By the first week in September I usually will have harvested most of my several hundred bean varieties. So, unless you're at a latitude or an elevation where there are fewer than 100 frost-free days, don't let concerns about getting dry beans to mature thwart your desire to grow them.

I've made it my business to popularize dried beans because my family and I have been increasingly impressed by their versatility and food value as well as their easy culture and storage. If you are interested in becoming protein self-sufficient, growing dried beans is an excellent place to start. I have found dozens of high-yielding, short-season and great-tasting dried beans that are not offered by stores or seed companies. As with almost all homegrown food, your own dried beans will taste better than store-bought varieties. Not only are garden-grown beans more easily digested, they also demand you highlight rather than bury their taste under condiments and spices. In time, you may become so intimate with the nuance and bounty of bean flavours that you'll reach for Montezuma Reds, Norwegians or Ireland Creek Annies with as much authority and discernment as you now have for cheddar, Swiss or Camembert cheese!

Varieties

Beans are divided into snap, shell and dry varieties depending on their stage of development at harvest. Snap beans, also called string, green or yellow beans, are picked fresh from early summer on, when their seeds are still undeveloped or very small. Shell beans, also called horticultural beans, are harvested when the beans are fully formed in the pods but not dried out. Dry beans are harvested when they rattle in the pods.

There is some overlapping of the types: some snap beans and most horticultural beans can be left to mature into quite good dry beans, and some dry beans are quite tasty at the green shell stage. Most dry beans also make good green beans if picked early enough. Dry beans, if picked as green or yellow snaps, will likely have strings: snap off the head and tail of the bean, and the string will come along, too.

You'll want to consider whether to choose a bush or a pole variety of dry bean. Pole beans grow two to three metres (six to ten feet) tall by twining around sticks, strings or wires; strong supports, such as trellises or tepees, are best set in place before or soon after the seeds are sown. Bush types are self-supporting and grow only to 60 or 90 centimetres (two or three feet). As far as flavour is concerned, there are many delicious varieties of both pole and bush beans.

Soil Preference

Beans are very easy to grow. Though they are at their best in moderately rich soil, they do well in a wide range of soils, even without fertilizer. In especially acidic soil (below a pH of 6) the addition of bonemeal, wood ashes, dolomite lime or compost will, by their alkaline nature, moderate the acidity. In a very sandy soil that leaches nutrients easily, organic nitrogen products should be added, but bear in mind that too much will promote excessive leaf growth, and delay and reduce pod production.

Nitrogen is important for good bean growth, but because they're legumes beans can fix their own nitrogen from the air through the action of the *Rhizobium* bacteria that live in nodules on their roots. Thus beans are an excellent crop for enriching your soil. In a new garden, however, it's worth coating your bean seed with an inoculant containing the proper type of *Rhizobium*, carried at most garden shops, to ensure its presence. Once these bacteria are in the soil, they multiply rapidly and persist indefinitely. Soybeans have a bacteria inoculant specific to them, as do other legumes.

There is another consideration to note when choosing a planting site for dry beans. Green and shell beans are usually harvested when the summer sun is still high.

Because dry beans take about six weeks longer to reach full maturity and because you want to harvest their pods at maximum dryness, plant them where they will continue to receive sun on August and September afternoons.

Planting Time

Most catalogues and gardening books suggest planting beans just after the last estimated spring frost date. On the coast here, where the last frost occurs in March or even February but the soil does not warm quickly, I wait until at least early May to ensure good, even germination. Beans are a warm-weather crop and there is little to be gained by having them shiver through their early growth. On a small scale, planting beans in raised beds saves a lot of space and work. Raised beds also heat more quickly in spring to allow an earlier sowing. Soaking beans beforehand is not usually worth it when they are going into cold soil anyway. Because presoaking often results in cracked seed and more difficult sowing, I recommend it only for late-season starts.

Sowing

Planting my dry beans in rows 45 centimetres (18 inches) apart allows me to do most of my weeding by rototilling between the rows until the bean plants fill the open areas and block out weeds. I sow the seed about 2.5 centimetres (one inch) deep, using a push row seeder (an efficient and inexpensive tool for large gardens), and later thin the seedlings to a few centimetres apart to allow for adequate air circulation around the plants.

Maintenance

Bean diseases seldom ruin a backyard harvest. During the 20-odd years I've been growing beans on Salt Spring Island, I've seen no bean diseases and only a few aphids and bean beetles. It is worth taking precautions, however. Don't risk spreading rusts, mildews or blights by working among wet plants. Remove or turn under bean debris when the plants are finished. Gardening guides recommend rotating the location of the bean crop from year to year for disease and pest management. However, I break that rule on occasion and usually get better harvests thanks to the abundance of nitrogen-fixing bacteria still in the soil from the previous crop.

Dry beans aren't "dry" until three to four months after planting, so until then the main tasks are watering, weeding or mulching, and watching for insects or disease. Most bush beans help keep the soil from drying out by their spreading habit. Mulch, if available, can greatly reduce the need to water and weed. The most crucial time to ensure adequate soil moisture is during pod and seed formation; fewer and smaller beans will result if the plants stay thirsty at this time. Other than that, beans are fairly drought-tolerant.

Harvesting

With short-season varieties, anyone blessed with a hot, sunny site can have a crop that dries to perfection in the garden. The leaves fall off the plants and the pods turn brown. On hot late-summer days, the pods start spilling their beans. Pick them before too many have fallen. To ensure that the pods are thoroughly dry, bring them indoors to a warm, dry place with good air circulation. Some varieties ripen over a week or two, and it's often best to go through the patch every few days to pick the driest.

If you're experimenting with different varieties, you'll find that many longer-season beans do not reach the drying stage until September or October, when rain and fog are common. If the weather is dismal, pull entire plants and hang them upside down in a well-ventilated greenhouse, shed, barn, attic or basement. Do this also if frost threatens, as bean plants are killed by only a few degrees of frost. So long as the crop is close to maturity, the seeds will continue to ripen in the pods even after they've been removed from the plant. Even relatively immature beans may ripen this way. If the pods are damp when picked but the weather is clear, spread them on tarps in a sunny place to prevent the growth of mould. If they are already dry, bring the pods indoors and stir them occasionally until the beans reach their full colour.

Threshing

I used to place the dry pods on waist-high tables in a greenhouse and at the end of one or two hot days I would thresh them by hand in a matter of minutes. The method is actually closer to kneading than threshing; squeezing and cracking the dry pods with the fingers, the shelled beans quickly go to the bottom and the split pods stay on top. An alternative and quite enjoyable method of shelling the pods (my preferred method now) is to place them in my threshing box and to then walk/shuffle over them. You can use any large box, chest or trough. It is most important in this case that the beans be totally dry or they will be crushed.

I once cleaned threshed beans by putting them in a large bowl outdoors and then blowing away the chaff with a hair dryer. All the while, I screened out any debris or weed seeds and discarded any mouldy or discoloured beans by hand. Then I discovered the air compressor, previously reserved for filling truck and tractor tires. The right nozzle attachment and degree of pressure directed at my bucket of beans got the job done in a few minutes.

Storage

When beans are sufficiently dry, a thumbnail cannot dent them. Some catalogues recommend putting beans in the freezer for a few days to kill any bean weevils that could damage the crop in storage, but I have yet to find any of the small holes in beans that are the telltale signs of weevils. If you decide to follow the freezing procedure, give the beans a little extra drying after removing them, as beans placed in the freezer collect some moisture. Store dried beans in labelled jars on a cool, dry shelf.

Yield

Yield is a significant consideration when choosing varieties. For example, a 15-metre (50-foot) row of Jacob's Cattle beans usually provides half the 3.5 to 4.5 kilograms (eight or 10 pounds) of dry beans I'd harvest from another variety. However, yield is determined by many factors: many of my far-flung seed customers to whom I have sent Jacob's Cattle beans report harvests of more than 4.5 kilograms (10 pounds) per same row length.

I have occasionally had early and abundant yields from supermarket dry beans, especially navy and kidney beans.

If you save and plant seed from your earliest and highest-yielding plants, you'll have your own locally adapted strain in a few years. Once you have a type you like that does well for you, you need never purchase seed again.

Yield is sometimes not as important as taste or beauty. Many dry beans are particularly delicious or so pretty that a child's delight in shelling them might overshadow the importance of quantity.

Cooking

Common beans I've mentioned are indigenous to the Western Hemisphere. They were introduced to Europe in the 16th and 17th centuries, later to return to North America. Most of the world's cuisines have wonderful bean-based dishes, but in Central and South America it's been beans for 7,000 years!

Cooked dry beans are delicious in a wide variety of main and side dishes. They are a nourishing, versatile staple, each kind with its own flavour and texture.

The flatulence factor in beans is a major concern for many people. One tested method for reducing gas caused by beans is to change the soaking water two or three times, replenishing the pot with fresh water each time. Rinsing beans after they've been soaked also removes gas-promoting substances. Cooking beans thoroughly is important: uncooked starch is obviously harder to digest. Do not add baking soda as some books suggest: it reduces flavour and nutrition by making the water too alkaline, it can toughen the beans, and it doesn't lessen the offending substances. Do not add salt to the soaking or cooking water: it reacts with the seed coat and prevents absorption of liquids. Beyond these precautions, the best way to avoid flatulence is to cook homegrown beans: chemical changes transpire as beans age, making them less digestible when cooked.

Homegrown beans do not need as much soaking or cooking as do purchased beans. The usual recommendation of an overnight soaking is for convenience and also because some beans will have been lying around for years. Relatively fresh beans absorb all the water they can in four hours. Use three or four times as much water as beans. If you don't have time for a long soak, place washed and sorted beans in a large pot, cover them with three or four times their volume of fresh water, heat and hold them at a boil for two minutes. Then remove the pot from the heat and leave it covered for an hour. Rinse the beans and they will be ready to cook. The final product will not be as mellow as it should be, because beans have a better texture if they absorb water slowly; nevertheless, the loss of nutrients from the quick-soaking method is negligible.

After four hours of soaking, most homegrown beans need 50 minutes of cooking. (Soybeans and favas need about 90 minutes.) To cook presoaked beans in a pot, cover them with fresh, cold water, bring to a boil, reduce heat, partially cover the pot to prevent foaming and simmer for the indicated length of time. When using a pressure cooker, make sure the pot is no more than half full and cook at seven kilograms (15 pounds) pressure for 15 to 25 minutes. Some beans, especially soybeans, have a tendency to bubble up through the pressure valve during cooking. To prevent this, add a tablespoonful of vegetable oil per cup of beans before cooking. Oil also helps reduce foam when using a conventional saucepan.

The texture of cooked beans can greatly enhance their appeal, so it's important to know how long to cook them. Cooking them for just under an hour leaves most of the beans I grow with a little chewiness to complement their taste. Pressure-cooked beans inevitably have a soft-textured inside and a tender skin. Do not cook beans in a sauce in an effort to soften and flavour them at the same time: many ingredients tend to halt the tenderizing process. When you add cooked beans to a sauce, their texture will not change but they will happily absorb the new flavours.

Saving Seed

Common beans are self-fertile, so it is rare to see any crosses. However, some cultivars have a more open flower than others, enabling the occasional fertilization by insects. To maintain pure strains it is advisable to separate varieties by a row of another plant species or to grow late-maturing beans beside ones with an earlier maturity.

Runner beans, such as Scarlet Runners, are a different species and cultivars will cross. If growing two or more runner beans, separate them as much as possible if seed purity is desired.

Genetically Modified?

It is still safe to buy regular whole beans in markets or from seed companies.

Outlook

The recent rise in popularity of dried beans is bound to accelerate as more and more people discover how tasty and digestible they can be. Beans also have tons going for them in terms of contributing to healthy bodies and a healthy planet.

Degenerative diseases are almost unheard of where diets include large quantities of beans and other fibre foods. As cultures replace beans and other complex carbohydrates with foods loaded with fats and cholesterol, there is a corresponding increase in cardiovascular diseases, intestinal ailments, cancers of the digestive system, appendicitis, gallstones, diverticulosis, hiatus hernia, hemorrhoids and diabetes.

Beans are a boon to diabetics, hypoglycemics and those on weight-loss diets. Only two to six percent of the calories in beans are derived from fat, in contrast to 75 to 85 percent for meat and cheese. Not only are they cholesterol-free, beans don't trigger a rise in blood sugar or require that the pancreas pour out extra insulin to readjust the glucose level in the blood.

Beans are high in protein and are well endowed with thiamine, niacin, B-6 and folic acid as well as calcium, iron, phosphorous and potassium. The fibre in beans helps keep the digestive system clean and promotes regularity.

It takes seven kilograms (16 pounds) of feed and 11,300 litres (2,500 gallons) of water to produce one pound of beef. Why grow beans to prepare millions of animals for slaughter when we could be eating them ourselves for better health, nutrition and agriculture.

Dry beans don't have to be refrigerated, frozen, canned or packaged in plastic. Between 22 and 44 times less fossil fuel is required to produce beans (and grains, for that matter) rather than meat.

RECIPES

beans

NAKED BEANS

When I'm taste-testing a new bean variety, I always try the beans without any adornment. I cover them in fresh, cold water for four or more hours, change the water, heat them to boiling point, then simmer them for 50 minutes until tender. Most of the beans I test this way are a delicious treat, savoured by my family, bean by bean.

The cooking water from homegrown beans makes excellent soup stock.

SCANDINAVIAN BEANS

SERVES 2–3

A traditional northern European method of preparing brown beans is almost as simple as the previous recipe.

1 CUP	DRY BEANS	250 ML
1/2 TBSP	OIL OR BUTTER	7.5 ML
2 TBSP	BROWN SUGAR, HONEY OR MOLASSES	30 ML
1 TBSP	CIDER VINEGAR	15 ML
	SALT TO TASTE	

After soaking the beans, heat them to boiling and simmer until tender. Drain and add the remaining ingredients. Serve hot.

Some people add a cinnamon stick or two to the cooking beans.

You can create your own sweet-bean recipe by adding preferred proportions of grated apple and/or carrot and including some ketchup or tomato sauce, minced garlic and summer savory.

Sweet Baked Beans

Serves 2–4

Many delicious bean dishes that are baked in the oven rather than cooked on the stove top use only a few ingredients. They usually involve sautéing onions with seasonings before mixing with cooked beans in a casserole, as in the following recipe.

1 CUP	DRY BEANS, SOAKED	250 ML
2 TBSP	OIL	30 ML
1	LARGE ONION, SLICED	1
1/2 TSP	DRY MUSTARD	2 ML
3 TBSP	HONEY OR MAPLE SYRUP	45 ML
	OR	
1 TBSP	MOLASSES	15 ML
SALT AND PEPPER TO TASTE		

Cook the beans. Drain and reserve the liquid.

Sauté the onion in the oil until translucent. Stir in the mustard and honey, salt and pepper. Add the beans and enough of their cooking liquid to barely cover. Transfer to a casserole dish and bake, covered, at 180°C (350°F) for 40 to 50 minutes. Remove the lid for an additional 10 to 15 minutes to reduce liquid, if necessary.

The seasonings in this recipe can be varied to complement specific bean varieties. For instance, for red kidneys, one and a half tablespoons of paprika can be used instead of the mustard and honey in the above. An additional sliced onion and a bay leaf in the casserole while the kidneys are baking would fill out this dish better.

If using pinto beans, a couple of cloves of crushed or finely chopped garlic can highlight the spiciness of the pintos. The garlic can be sautéed with the onions or (for a more powerful garlic effect) added directly to the casserole.

This above recipe also works well with dry limas.

BLACK BEAN EXPRESS

SERVES 4

The hearty taste of black beans is complemented rather than camouflaged by the ingredients in this simple recipe.

1 CUP	DRY BLACK BEANS	250 ML
1 TBSP	COOKING OIL	15 ML
1 TSP	GINGER, FRESHLY GRATED	5 ML
1/2 TSP	CUMIN	2 ML
2	GARLIC CLOVES, CHOPPED FINE	2
3	LEEKS, CHOPPED	3
1 TBSP	MISO	15 ML
1 TSP	MOLASSES	5 ML
1/4 CUP	PARSLEY, CHOPPED	60 ML

Soak the beans overnight or for a minimum of four hours. Cover beans with at least twice the volume of fresh, cold water, and add oil. Heat to boiling and simmer for 90 minutes.

In a skillet over medium heat, cook the ginger, cumin and garlic for several minutes. Add leeks and sauté until golden.

Dilute the miso in a small amount of warm water and combine with molasses.

Combine everything with the drained soybeans and cook on stove top for 20 minutes. Shortly before serving, stir in parsley.

Serve with a cooked grain.

THANKSGIVING BEANS

SERVES 6–8

This dish is especially festive if the main ingredients are fresh from the garden.

1 CUP	DRIED BEANS	250 ML
1/4 CUP	COOKING OIL	60 ML
4	MEDIUM ONIONS, COARSELY CHOPPED	4
2 TBSP	GARLIC, CHOPPED	30 ML
6 CUP	ITALIAN PLUM TOMATOES, CHOPPED	1.5 L
1	MEDIUM-SIZED WINTER SQUASH, COOKED	1
1 TBSP	GREEN OR RED CHILI OR	15 ML
	JALAPEÑO PEPPERS, FINELY CHOPPED	
2 TBSP	ORANGE RIND, CHOPPED	30 ML
1/2 CUP	RAISINS	125 ML
1/2 TSP	CINNAMON	2 ML
1/2 TSP	ALLSPICE	2 ML
1/2 TSP	NUTMEG	2 ML
1/4 TSP	GROUND CLOVES	1 ML
2	LARGE TART APPLES, PEELED,	2
	CORED AND CUBED	
	SALT AND FRESHLY GROUND PEPPER TO TASTE	

Soak the beans for four hours. Heat to boiling in a large pot and simmer for one hour.

Sauté onions and garlic in oil in a large skillet until golden. Stir in tomatoes, squash, peppers, orange rind, raisins and spices and simmer uncovered for 20 to 30 minutes.

Stir in drained beans and apples. Simmer for 10 minutes.

Serve with oven-roasted potatoes.

THREE-BEAN SALAD

SERVES 4–6

This variation of a traditional salad is greatly enhanced by the colours, textures and freshness inherent in homegrown beans. It can include as many varieties as you like. Red and white kidney beans with black garbanzos or black soybeans make an appealing combination.

1 1/2 CUPS	DRY BEANS	375 ML
1/2 CUP	LEEKS, SHALLOTS OR CHIVES, MINCED	125 ML
6 TBSP	OLIVE OIL	90 ML
2 TBSP	FRESH LEMON JUICE	30 ML
2 TBSP	DILL OR BASIL, CHOPPED	30 ML
1/2 TSP	TAMARI	2 ML
	PINCH OF CAYENNE PEPPER	
	SALT TO TASTE	

Soak beans in separate pots for a minimum of four hours. Heat to boiling and simmer until desired texture is reached. Drain and chill.

Thoroughly mix all ingredients in a bowl.

Make appealing individual servings by putting half a cup or more of the mixture on to romaine or other leaf lettuce. Garnish with a lemon wedge, a sprig of parsley, fresh dill, chervil or chive flowers.

BEAN AND BARLEY SOUP

SERVES 4

1	ONION, SLICED	1
2 TBSP	COOKING OIL	30 ML
1	CELERY STALK, DICED	1
2	CARROTS, DICED	2
3 CUPS	STOCK OR WATER	750 ML
1 CUP	BEANS, SOAKED	250 ML
2–3 TBSP	WHOLE BARLEY	30–45 ML
1 TBSP	FAVOURITE POWDERED HERBS	15 ML
	SALT AND PEPPER TO TASTE	

Cook the onion in the oil over medium heat until lightly browned. Add the celery and the carrots. Cover with the stock and add the beans and barley. Bring to the boil, then simmer for 50 minutes. Add the seasonings and simmer for an additional 30 minutes.

A few cloves of garlic, sautéed along with the other vegetables, impart a richer flavour to this soup. Finely chopped chervil makes a nice garnish.

BLACK BEANS AND RICE

SERVES 6–8

Cooked beans can be added to everything from soups to stews, pizzas to salads, casseroles to side dishes. They can be mashed with potatoes and squash. They go well with rice in this traditional dish.

2 CUPS	BLACK BEANS, COOKED	500 ML
2 CUPS	BROWN RICE, COOKED	500 ML
2 TBSP	OIL	30 ML
1	ONION, CHOPPED FINE	1
2	GARLIC CLOVES, CHOPPED FINE	2
1	SWEET PEPPER	1
	OR	
1	CELERY STALK, CHOPPED FINE	1
1 TSP	GROUND CUMIN	5 ML
1 TSP	DRIED OREGANO	5 ML
2–4	TOMATOES, COARSELY CHOPPED	2–4

Heat oil over medium-high heat. Sauté onion, garlic, pepper, cumin and oregano, stirring frequently until onion is translucent. Add tomatoes and cook, stirring for three to four minutes until well-blended. Turn heat to low. Stir in beans and cover, simmering gently for 15 minutes. Mound hot cooked rice on serving plate and create a well in the centre for the beans.

If using red instead of black beans, two to three teaspoons of chopped fresh basil (one or so if dried) makes a good substitute for cumin.

Pesto Soup

One's pesto reserves are great to utilize in bean soups. Pesto can also be made while brewing up the following:

1/2 CUP	MILD-FLAVOURED BEANS, SOAKED	125 ML
4 CUPS	WATER	1 L
1	ONION, CHOPPED	1
1 TBSP	COOKING OIL	15 ML
3	TOMATOES, CHOPPED	3
3	CARROTS, DICED	3
1	LEEK, CHOPPED	1
1	STALK OF CELERY, CHOPPED	1
2	POTATOES, DICED	2
2	ZUCCHINI, DICED	2
1 CUP	GREEN BEANS, SLICED	250 ML
	BROKEN SPAGHETTI, UNCOOKED	
Pesto: 3	GARLIC CLOVES	3
2 TBSP	FRESH BASIL, CHOPPED	30 ML
3 TBSP	TOMATO PASTE	45 ML
1/2 CUP	GRATED Parmesan CHEESE	125 ML
2 TBSP	OLIVE OIL	30 ML

Cook the beans in the water. Drain and reserve liquid. In a large soup pot, cook onion in oil until soft. Add tomatoes and cook for two minutes, while stirring. Add half the bean liquid, the carrots, leek, celery, potatoes, salt and pepper. Bring to a boil and simmer for 10 to 15 minutes.

Add zucchini, green beans and remaining liquid. Cook for five more minutes. Bring to a full boil and add spaghetti. Lower heat and simmer for 15 minutes.

Meanwhile, prepare the pesto by crushing the garlic and basil together in a mortar to a green paste. Blend in tomato paste and cheese. Add slowly until a thick paste results. (Alternatively, do all this in a blender or food processor.) Thin with two tablespoons of the stock. Serve in separate bowl so diners can add pesto to suit individual tastes.

CHAPTER SIX

Cool-Weather Beans
Favas, Garbanzos, Lentils and Peas

Although grown on a very large scale in North America, almost all favas, garbanzos, lentils and peas are produced for export or animal consumption.

These four legumes can be planted earlier than regular beans and are normally harvested in July or August. Few home gardeners in North America grow these for the bounty of dry beans they can produce but I predict their ascendence in the garden.

They are very attractive plants as well as being hardy, care-free crops. Their nitrogen-fixing ability enriches garden soil, as does the large quantity of organic matter they add when turned under. Favas, garbanzos, lentils and peas are nourishing, versatile and delicious foods that offer diverse and rewarding choices to the home gardener aiming for self-reliance.

Favas

Favas were grown by the ancient Egyptians and Chinese, as well as by the Greeks and Romans. They were a mainstay of the European diet until Columbus introduced warmer-weather beans. They are now eaten daily by millions of people in the Middle East, India, Burma, Mexico and Brazil.

Fava beans are a tenacious and trouble-free crop that succeeds where the growing season is short and other beans would fail — they survive temperatures as low as -14°C (6°F). They require minimal or no watering as long as there are good spring rains. They are easy to grow and produce abundantly.

Varieties

Some gardeners grow a large-seeded fava called the broad bean, which is shelled as a fresh bean. Unfortunately, most varieties of broad beans aren't good-tasting as a cooked dry bean. But some are. To my taste, the best favas are the small-seeded ones normally grown in North America as cover crops. These are usually referred to as tic or bell beans and have seeds more like large peas than the huge kidney shape of other favas.

Most cultivated favas grow from one to 1.5 metres (four to five feet), with succulent-looking blue-green leaves on squarish and pulpy stalks. Except for a single crimson-flowered variety, flowers are white with distinctive black centres. The pods that splay out from the stem vary considerably in length in cultivars, some being up to 30 centimetres (one foot). Some varieties have eight large, lima-size seeds per pod. Most varieties need the better part of four months to mature beans.

Planting Time

In coastal and southern areas, favas can be planted in spring or fall. They are hardier than peas, so if you can plant out peas in autumn you can plant out favas as well. In most of the continent, seeding as soon as the soil can be worked in spring should enable plants to mature beans. Light frost will not harm the young plants. Because fava blossoms will fall off before setting pods if temperatures go much above 21°C (70°F), they won't mature seeds in places where hot summers come on quickly. Strategies that prolong pea harvests also work for favas, such as planting in shadier areas, hilling soil around the base of plants, mulching and keeping the soil moist.

Soil Preference

Favas grow successfully in many different soils, even heavy clay. They shouldn't need fertilizer if grown in built-up garden soil. They do best in well-cultivated ground that is high in phosphorus and potassium and, like peas, they prefer soil that is not too acidic.

Sowing

Soaking the seeds overnight, though not necessary, ensures fast, even germination. In garden beds, the seeds should be planted one to two inches deep and four to six inches apart, in rows a foot or more apart.

Maintenance

These beans compete poorly with weeds until they start to tower above them and, in the early stages, can benefit considerably from mulching or from soil drawn around the base of the plants with a hoe or rake. All varieties I've tried so far haven't required support, but in windy places it might be worthwhile staking each end of the row and enclosing the beans with string.

Watering is seldom necessary with favas unless spring is unusually dry.

Favas are fairly pest- and disease-resistant. Their most common problem is aphids. Some writers suggest controlling aphid by using insecticidal soap or by pinching off plant tops. I find that aphids will usually congregate on a small percentage of plants and leave the rest alone.

Harvesting

Picked green — that is, as soon as the pods are well-formed and deep green — favas can be shelled and eaten fresh or cooked. The pods at the base of the stalk blacken first and farmers usually combine or cut field favas for silage when the two lowest pods have blackened. The home gardener wanting dry beans can wait to pick until half the pods have dried black, usually by the end of July. It takes several weeks for all the pods to dry, necessitating two or three pickings. The weather of late July and early August most often enables leisurely harvesting, but if left standing too long in hot weather the pods of some varieties will shatter and the beans fall to the ground.

When sufficiently dry, a fingernail won't dent the beans. They can be shelled by hand or threshed by foot in a box or on a tarp.

Yield

Bell beans yield up to 5.5 kilograms per 15 metres (12 pounds per 50 feet) while the larger seeded favas generally produce about three-quarters that amount.

Cooking

A few individuals, usually males of Mediterranean descent, experience a hereditary allergic reaction when they eat fresh (rather than dried) beans or inhale fava pollen. The symptoms of "favism" usually disappear without treatment within a few days of exposure. Where fava beans are a dietary staple, allergies to them are detected as a matter of course; in North America, the possibility of allergic reaction, though extremely slight, is worth bearing in mind.

Writers point out that favas need a long soaking and many hours' cooking. No doubt this is because most commercially available fava beans have aged and oxidized considerably before reaching the consumer. I have found that all the favas I've grown require about 90 minutes' simmering after an overnight soak. The seed coat retains a chewiness that is quite pleasant in some varieties but decidedly tough in others. The taste in the best varieties is rich, earthy and sweet, and easily the equal of any other kind of bean.

The taste of fresh green favas stewed or simmered is somewhere between that of peas and limas. They are too old for fresh use if a yellowish green skin has already formed. Green favas have as much protein as green limas, 10 times as much as snap beans and about a quarter more than fresh peas, plus more iron and potassium than any of these.

Dried favas average about 30 percent protein (compared with 40 percent for soybeans and 20 to 25 percent for most other dry beans); they contain very little oil but are high in carbohydrates.

Saving Seed

Favas are mostly self-fertile but can be cross-pollinated by insects. If you want to maintain pure strains, plant only one variety, stagger plantings or grow different cultivars as far apart in the garden as possible.

Genetically Modified?

No GM varieties are in the marketplace yet.

Outlook

Given that favas have been and continue to be popular in cultures around the globe, it seems they could easily catch on in North America as well. In areas where summers are warm but not too hot, or where winters are cool but not much below freezing, they are an incredibly hardy and prolific crop. A major drawback is the fact that seeds ripen unevenly over a period of several weeks, making combine harvesting somewhat inefficient. At the home-garden level, having to harvest more than once shouldn't be any more onerous than picking peas at different times. At the farm level, I think it's time to stop regarding labour-intensive harvesting as bad news, especially when the crop to be harvested is such good news!

Chick-peas and Lentils

Fine varieties of both chick-peas and lentils are readily and inexpensively available in the marketplace. Nevertheless, their easy cultivation makes them worthy of consideration in the food garden.

Chick-peas (also known as garbanzos)

Chick-peas have been grown in Mediterranean countries since as early as 8000 B.C. The Romans used the word *arietinum* (ram-like) to describe this bean because its roundish, compressed seed somewhat resembles a ram's head with horns curling over the sides. *Cicer arietinum* was a staple of their diet and still plays an important part in the regional cooking of southern Europe. Chick-peas are widely grown in India and Burma, where they rival wheat in acreage under cultivation. They are India's most important legume.

The chick-pea is a delicate, graceful plant that branches near the ground and is usually about 60 centimetres (two feet) high. One or two seeds are borne in numerous round, swollen pods about four months from the time of sowing.

Chick-peas are a cooler-weather crop and can be sown, like peas, early in spring. The plants are best thinned to about 30 centimetres apart because of their spreading habit. They don't need staking. They require little attention beyond the occasional weeding or hoeing and are quite drought-tolerant. The dry pods are more difficult to process than those of other beans: the shells have a lanolin-like stickiness and cave in rather than split apart when hand-threshed. I recommend you place them on a tarp on the ground or in a large container such as a box or an ice chest and "do the shuffle" over them.

If you've already prepared such specialty dishes as tabbouleh and hummus, you're in for a special treat when you prepare them with homegrown garbanzos. As with other fresh-grown beans, their taste is mild and sweet and cooking times are considerably less than is usually recommended. In this case, 90 minutes is sufficient after an overnight soaking (rather than two and a one-half hours).

The chick-pea is one of the more nutritious members of the bean family, rich in protein, calcium, iron and B vitamins.

Lentils

Lentils have been cultivated for 10,000 or more years. Lens is the Latin word for lentil, hence its coinage in the 17th century as the word for a doubly convex piece of glass shaped like a lentil. Lentils are enormously important in many countries, especially in Asia and north Africa.

Lentils are a small and very branching plant, forming a tuft just over 30 centimetres (one foot) high. The small white or pale blue flowers are produced in pairs and are succeeded by very flat pods, each of which usually contains two seeds. Lentils are closely related to peas and, like them, do best in cool, moist, sandy loam. They are hardy, easy-to-grow nitrogen-fixers that can be planted as soon as the soil is workable in the spring. Sow the seeds about one centimetre (half an inch) deep and 10 centimetres (four inches) apart.

Lentils are easily threshed by hand or foot. Crossing does not readily occur between different cultivars.

Lentils need no soaking and cook relatively quickly — from 10 to 40 minutes, depending on variety. They must be watched because, unlike chick-peas, they soften easily and can lose their texture. In the Middle East they are most often used in soups and stews and are frequently flavoured with lemon, olive oil and garlic. In south India, where they are a major source of protein, many methods are used to prepare lentils for breads, fritters, salads, pancakes and vegetable dishes. Lentils are 25 percent protein and are rich in iron and vitamin B.

Peas

Most people who grow peas don't think of allowing them to dry on the vine to be stored without processing until ready for use. Split peas cook faster than unprocessed whole peas, but other than that there is no reason to not celebrate dry whole peas. They are excellent cooked in many of the ways you would prepare lentils, chick-peas, favas or other beans, adding a rich creamy gravy and smoky flavour to winter dishes.

Soil Preference

Peas thrive in a well-drained rich, sandy, alkaline soil. Because they can rot in cold, wet ground it is often worthwhile, especially for early plantings, to hill soil somewhat under pea fencing or in pea beds. Peas will tolerate some shading.

Varieties

Peas are natural climbers but there are many low-growing ones that will support themselves with the help of their neighbours. Varieties over knee-high should be given some support or planted along a fence or trellis.

Varieties range from those with tiny round seeds to those with large, rectangular seeds. There is a major division between fresh-eating peas and those best used as a dry bean. Although most shelling peas aren't very good soup peas and vice versa, I have found many edible pod peas that are rich and flavourful when used in soups and curries. Some soup peas break down quickly to make a rich broth and some retain their shape to pleasing effect.

Planting Time

Peas generally can be sown as soon as the soil can be worked until June. August plantings for fall harvest can also succeed if the weather cooperates.

Sowing

As with other legumes, an application of garden inoculant, either to the soil or to the seeds themselves before planting, can be very beneficial. Sow seeds 2.5 centimetres (one inch) apart and 2.5 centimetres deep. Pea plants can tolerate crowding, so rows can be spaced as close as a few centimetres apart.

Maintenance

Peas are light feeders; if organic matter such as rotted manure, compost, leaf mould or old hay has been worked into the soil they should do very well.

It's best to weed peas well at the beginning, because once they get going it's hard to work between stalks without damaging the vines.

Peas like having wet feet and it is most important to maintain even moisture during flowering and pod set.

Harvesting

Dry peas are ready to harvest when the pods have dried.

Threshing

As with other legumes, peas are easily threshed by hand or foot and they should be dry enough so a fingernail can't make a mark.

Yield

Because peas tolerate crowding they are capable of very high yields. I've obtained up to eight kilograms per nine square metres (17 pounds per 100 square feet) from varieties broadcast in wide beds. Rows of fenced peas can provide more than 4.5 kilograms per nine square metres (10 pounds per 100 feet).

Cooking

Your own dry peas will take 60 to 90 minutes' simmering to soften. Varieties vary considerably in holding their texture and you may prefer shorter or longer cooking, depending on the kind of stew or soup you're preparing.

Saving Seed

Peas are self-fertile, so saving your own is simply a matter of keeping some of your harvest for the next planting. I have not seen any pea crosses in all the years I have been growing them.

Genetically Modified?

Genetically altered peas, lentils and favas have yet to appear in stores or from seed sources.

Outlook

Peas are a common item in most seed catalogues, yet few companies promote them as dry legumes. As with the other beans and grains in this book, there are many varieties that could expand and enhance our diets if we became aware of their potential. I think dry peas will become more popular as growers realize they don't have to be split to be usable: peas are already known as an easy, satisfying crop, and soup from your own peas need only be tried once to win converts.

RECIPES

cool–weather
beans

FAVA SOUP BEGINNING

Although 90 minutes' simmering after an overnight soaking is enough to cook homegrown favas, longer cooking will not render them mushy as it does other beans.

4 CUPS	COOKED FAVAS	1 L
1	LARGE ONION, CHOPPED	1
2	GARLIC CLOVES, MINCED	2
1	CARROT, GRATED	1

Combine favas with sautéed onion, garlic and carrot. Add additional water or tomato sauce, plain yogourt, spices and seasonings, then purée in blender. Reheat without boiling.

FAVA STEW

SERVES 5–6

4 CUPS	COOKED FAVAS	1 L
1/4 CUP	BUTTER OR OIL	60 ML
1	LARGE ONION, CHOPPED	1
1/2 CUP	GRATED CARROT	125 ML
1	CELERY STALK, DICED	1
2	GARLIC CLOVES, MINCED	2
1/2 CUP	ALL-PURPOSE FLOUR	125 ML
1/4 TSP	DRIED THYME	1 ML
	PINCH OF NUTMEG	
1 CUP	VEGETABLE OR GARLIC STOCK	250 ML
2	EGGS, WELL BEATEN	2
1/2 CUP	FRESH FRENCH SORREL, CHOPPED FINE	125 ML
1/2 CUP	KALE, CHOPPED FINE	125 ML
	SALT AND PEPPER TO TASTE	

Heat butter and sauté onion, carrot, celery and garlic for five to eight minutes. Stir in flour, thyme, salt, pepper and nutmeg. Gradually add stock and cook, stirring gently for 10 minutes. Turn down heat and stir in eggs slowly. Cook for a few more minutes and add sorrel, kale and cooked favas. Heat through and serve.

Ful Mesdames

Serves 3–4

This basic fava bean salad uses ingredients typical of Middle Eastern fava dishes and is traditionally served with hard-boiled eggs and parsley.

1/2 CUP	DRIED FAVA BEANS, SOAKED	125 ML
4 TBSP	OLIVE OR FLAX OIL	60 ML
	JUICE OF 1/2 LEMON	
2	GARLIC CLOVES, CRUSHED OR	2
	FINELY CHOPPED	

Cook beans until soft (about 90 minutes). Drain well. Dress with oil, lemon and garlic. Let cool.

Sprouted Chick-pea Salad

Serves 4–6

2 CUPS	CHICK-PEAS, SPROUTED	500 ML
2	GARLIC CLOVES, FINELY CHOPPED	2
1/4 CUP	CHOPPED CHIVES OR SCALLIONS	60 ML
1	TOMATO, DICED	1
1/4 CUP	FRESH PARSLEY, CHOPPED	60 ML
2 TBSP	WINE VINEGAR OR LEMON JUICE	30 ML
1/2 CUP	OLIVE OIL	125 ML
	SEA SALT AND FRESHLY GROUND	
	BLACK PEPPER TO TASTE	

Combine all ingredients and toss to mix. Can be served on a bed of salad greens.

LOVING KINDNESS HUMMUS

SERVES 4

1 CUP	CHICK-PEAS	250 ML
1	CARROT, LARGE	1
3	GARLIC CLOVES (OR MORE)	3
1	BAY LEAF	1
2	LEMONS, JUICED	2
1/2 CUP	SESAME TAHINI	125 ML
	SALT TO TASTE	

Soak chick-peas in 750 millilitres (three cups) of cold water for at least four hours. Rinse and add fresh water to cover. Simmer for 90 minutes with coarsely chopped carrot, whole peeled garlic cloves and bay leaf, until very tender. Drain, reserving cooking liquid.

Remove bay leaf and mash the rest while still hot. Stir in the lemon juice, tahini and crushed or finely chopped garlic. Add small amounts of cooking liquid until desired moistness is reached. Salt to taste.

Serve with whole-grain crackers or pita bread as an appetizer or snack. Makes good lunch sandwiches, too.

Try this recipe with favas, lentils or peas instead of chick-peas, varying soaking and cooking times appropriately.

BASIC LENTILS

Although lentils don't need it, overnight soaking will decrease cooking time somewhat. Depending on the variety, lentils can take anywhere from 20 minutes to an hour to cook. Simmer with a bay leaf in three times their volume of water. When cooked and drained, add a little oil or butter and lemon juice. Season with paprika, pepper, soy sauce, et cetera and remove the bay leaf.

SWEET-AND-SOUR LENTILS

SERVES 4

1 CUP	DRIED LENTILS	250 ML
2 CUPS	VEGETABLE STOCK	500 ML
1	BAY LEAF	1
1	GARLIC CLOVE, FINELY CHOPPED	1
1/8 TSP	GROUND CLOVES	.5 ML
1/8 TSP	NUTMEG	.5 ML
3 TBSP	OIL	45 ML
3 TBSP	APPLE CIDER OR JUICE	45 ML
3 TBSP	CIDER VINEGAR	45 ML
3 TBSP	HONEY, MOLASSES OR SUGAR	45 ML
	SALT TO TASTE	

Bring the stock to a boil in a large pot and add the lentils, bay leaf and salt. Cover and simmer gently for 30 minutes. Add remaining ingredients. Stir to mix well. Cook for five minutes longer, or until lentils are tender.

GWEN MALLARD'S PEA SOUP

1/2 CUP	BARLEY	125 mL
2 CUPS	DRIED SOUP PEAS	500 mL
2 TBSP	OLIVE OIL	30 mL
12 CUPS	BOILING WATER	3 L
1	LARGE ONION, CHOPPED	1
1/4	MEDIUM CABBAGE, CHOPPED	1/4
2	MEDIUM POTATOES, DICED	2
2	LARGE CARROTS, DICED	2
	FRESH HERBS, CHOPPED TO TASTE	
	SALT TO TASTE	

Place barley, peas, oil and salt in a large pot. Pour boiling water over ingredients and simmer gently, stirring frequently to prevent sticking. Cook for about two hours or until peas are at the purée stage. Add vegetables and cook slowly until tender without overcooking. Add salt and favourite herbs. This soup thickens as it stands and requires water when reheated.

CURRIED PEAS

SERVES 3–4

1 CUP	WHOLE DRY PEAS	250 ML
1	ONION CHOPPED	1
1	GARLIC CLOVE, CHOPPED	1
2 TBSP	OIL	30 ML
1–2 TSP	CURRY POWDER	5–10 ML
1/2 TSP	GROUND CUMIN	2 ML
2–3 CUPS	WATER	500–750 ML
1 TSP	SALT	5 ML
1 TBSP	GINGER, FRESHLY GRATED (OPTIONAL)	15 ML

Sauté the onion and garlic in oil. Add the curry and cumin and sauté for one minute longer. Add a little water if too dry. Add the peas and then the water, according to how much sauce you like. Add the salt and ginger, if desired. Bring to a boil and cook over very low heat for one hour.

CHAPTER SEVEN

Hot-Weather Beans:
Soybeans, Limas, Teparies, Adzukis

Soybeans

Soybeans were my first "discovery" and led to the creation of Salt Spring Seeds in 1986. I was amazed to find that some varieties of soybeans were tasty and digestible when cooked as a dry bean and that the growing season was long enough for them here in coastal British Columbia. In getting carried away by a host of other beans and grains since then, my initial enthusiasm for soybeans hasn't diminished but it has not been foremost in my mind. Now soybeans have returned to a prominent place in my thoughts, thanks to the recent acceleration of biogenetic engineering.

Monsanto Company has bioengineered a soybean that can withstand applications of their product Roundup. Roundup is the best-selling herbicide worldwide and basically kills any green living thing. To my mind, there is a qualitative difference between a soybean with extra genes inserted to render it immune to such a powerful poison and the original soybean. The company's officials dismiss such concerns as unscientific, but I say their attempts to push Roundup Ready Soybeans on us are very scary.

Although we don't know what transgenic crops might do to us or to the environment, their introduction into the marketplace is virtually unregulated. The North American public is denied the right to know if foods have been genetically modified. Sixty percent of food products contain processed soybeans and over 60 percent of cultivated soybeans in North America are now Roundup Ready. So the majority of people in North America are already part of Monsanto's monopoly game.

I've been glad to maintain some fine soybean varieties because they have a lot going for them as simple and nourishing food. Now the pleasure is tempered by necessity: the thought that Salt Spring Seeds might become one of the few sources of unmodified seed is a most sobering one.

Soybeans have been cultivated for over 5,000 years, most notably in China and Japan. Unfortunately, we process this wonderful legume in every imaginable fashion instead of simply cooking it up. Most accessible varieties have been bred for fodder or for processing rather than human consumption. The wonder is that there are delicious soybean varieties that grow as easily as the indigestible ones you may have already tried and rejected.

Vast acreages of soybeans are grown as fodder for cattle and pigs. The heavily subsidized meat and dairy industries wreak ecological havoc with both our water and soil resources. My question is, why grow soybeans to feed animals to feed people when we could be growing the beans to eat directly?

Soybeans are the only legume containing all nine essential amino acids (the only proteins the human body can't manufacture on its own). Soybeans have no cholesterol and are low in saturated fats and sodium. They are an excellent source of dietary fibre. They are high in iron, calcium, B vitamins, zinc, lecithin, phosphorus and magnesium.

(However, it is important to note that a lot of this goodness in lost or diminished by processing soybeans. Tofu, for example, contains 28 percent less iron, only 10 percent of the fibre and B vitamins and none of the vitamins A and C found in cooked whole soybeans.)

Soybeans contain approximately 40 percent protein by weight — more than any other unprocessed plant or animal food. A half hectare of soybeans produces between 10 and 20 times more usable protein than a half hectare grown to graze beef cattle. Despite the exaggeration of protein needs in North America, high-protein crops are more necessary as it becomes increasingly expensive and dangerous to eat at the top of the food chain. Even commercial non-GMO soybeans are relatively free of chemical toxins (though they have been sprayed with Roundup). Meat, fish and poultry have about 20 times and dairy foods about four and one-half times more pesticide residues than soybeans. Similarly, soybeans contain fewer radioactive residues and no synthetic hormone additives.

The drought tolerance of soybeans is a special asset, as it is very evident that water will become a most precious resource in the coming decades. Nor are soybeans heavy feeders; they require minimal fertilizer and are nitrogen-fixing plants that enrich the soil. The fact that soybeans can be simply cooked and eaten keeps energy output minimal. Freezing and canning are unnecessary, as are fancy plastic packages.

Soil Preference

A loose, well-drained loam is what soybeans like best, but they do well in a wide range of soil conditions. They prefer soil on the acidic side (pH from 5.8 to 7).

Varieties

Brown and black soybeans have the best flavour, but it is hard to find these except through a few seed companies. Yellow cultivars found in grocery and health-food stores are hard to digest and take forever to cook. Soybeans have long been known to contain many anticancer factors and recent research has shown that black soybeans are much higher in those factors than other soybeans.

Butterbean soybeans are used at the shell stage when the seeds have plumped the pods. Steam the unshelled pods for five minutes, put them under cold water, squeeze the beans out and reheat them briefly. They are a taste sensation in July and August, and they freeze well for year-round pleasure.

Planting Time

Soybeans are a warm-weather crop, usually planted at around the same time as corn. Soil and air temperatures of at least 10 to 16°C (55 to 60°F) are needed for good germination. The last week in May or the first week in June are the usual times to plant soybeans in southern Canada and the northern United States.

Sowing

I plant my seeds about 2.5 centimetres (one inch) deep in rows that are 30 to 60 centimetres (one to two feet) apart. Seeds should be able to absorb enough moisture to germinate, so if soil is low in moisture or sandy then plant twice as deep. Soybeans do well either in raised beds or in traditional rows. Although I space my soybeans 12 to

15 centimetres (five to six inches) apart so there is enough distance to safely hoe between them, they are fine at even five centimetres (two inches) apart. If you use a rototiller, it is most efficient to plant rows slightly more than a rototiller's width apart.

Like other legumes, soybeans have roots hosting nodule-forming bacteria that can convert the nitrogen in the air to a plant-usable kind. If soybeans have not been grown in your soil before, it is a good idea to inoculate the seed with the proper strain of nitrogen-fixing bacteria, available at farm and garden stores or through seed catalogues.

Maintenance

It is important to weed in the early stages, as soybeans can be much slower to get going than the common weeds that love June weather. I usually hoe and hand weed two or three times before the soybean plants form a canopy that shades out competition.

Reaching deep into the ground, soybeans have a fairly pronounced taproot that makes them quite tolerant of drought. The most important time to ensure adequate soil moisture is from flowering in early summer through pod formation shortly after.

In the dozen or more years I've been growing soybeans, I've had no problems with pests or diseases. I do turn my crops under every year and I wait four years before I grow them again in an area where they were previously planted.

Harvesting

Soybeans are ready to harvest as dry beans when the leaves have fallen and the beans rattle in their pods. This is usually around mid-September here on the West Coast, but early September where summers are hot. Pods can be picked individually. They can also be quickly stripped from the stalk with an upward motion of one hand. (Wear gloves, and hold the stalk lower down with the other hand.) I usually gather my harvest in large buckets.

Threshing

Pods can be shelled one by one or rubbed apart by foot in a threshing box. To thresh by foot, the seeds must be dry enough that a fingernail can't make an indentation. Chaff can be removed with suitable screening or blown away with a fan or hair dryer; I use a small air compressor with a blow-nozzle attachment. I always leave my seeds on screens in the sunlight for an extra day or two to ensure maximum drying.

Yield

Yields aren't as high as for other beans, but soybeans are a much more substantial food. A 30-metre (100-foot) row will fill a 4.5-litre (one-gallon) jar with about 3.5 kilograms (eight pounds) of soybeans. Intensive raised beds can yield almost two kilograms (more than four pounds) per three square metres (36 square feet).

Cooking

Homegrown soybeans need about 90 minutes' simmering after an overnight soaking to be cooked al dente. Most commercial types will need at least three hours' cooking.

Soybeans can be substituted for other dried beans in many recipes. They are more filling than pintos or kidneys because they are higher in both protein and oil. For this reason, when substituting soybeans for other legumes you can reduce the required amount by one-third.

Saving Seed

Soybean varieties don't cross, so maintaining your own seed is easy: don't eat all you harvest.

Genetically Modified?

Most soybeans and products made from them and with them are genetically modified. Look for certified organic seeds and products that are identified as GMO-free.

Outlook

Over 5 billion bushels of soybeans are harvested annually in North America, virtually none of which is intended for direct human consumption. If soybeans are ever to catch on as beans that can be eaten and appreciated like pinto or kidney beans, it seems to me that people who grow their own will be the ones to start the trend and create the demand. Soybeans do present such a great advertisement for themselves. The plants radiate a clean solidity, a robustness and a lushness that are consummated by the satisfaction of eating the mild and nutty cooked beans. They are a sustainable, delicious and totally appropriate food plant for our current and future sustenance. Try them — you'll love them!

Limas, Teparies and Adzukis

Limas, teparies and adzukis like it hot: they generally need a little more heat and/or a little more time to mature than do soybeans. I grow them successfully every year but I don't usually harvest them until early October, from a late-May sowing. Gardeners with a long, hot growing season can add these beans to the list of delectable, easily grown legumes.

Varieties

These are all bush beans, although there are pole limas as well as bush ones. Limas make wonderful fresh beans but I'm interested in them, as with the others, mainly as a dry bean. There are some great-tasting tepary, lima and adzuki beans to grow that you wouldn't be able to buy as food.

Soil Preference

All thrive in ordinary garden soil, are quite drought-tolerant and prefer good drainage. Tepary beans do well even in alkaline and salty soil.

Planting Time

Planting time is normally the same time as corn, when the ground has warmed considerably. Adzuki and tepary beans are quite small compared with kidneys and pintos, so will germinate more quickly under the right conditions.

Sowing

Direct seed about 2.5 centimetres (one inch) deep for limas, half that for the others. Seeds can also be soaked and germinated indoors if care is taken to not damage the sprouts when planting. Plants are quite sprawling and should be thinned to 15 centimetres (6 inches) apart in rows 45 to 90 centimetres (18 to 36 inches) apart.

Maintenance

As with other beans, weeding is important until the plants form a canopy. These beans will require minimal watering except in very dry conditions. Tepary and lima beans turn yellow when overwatered.

Harvesting

Harvest pods as they dry: mature pods will pop open and drop their seeds. If it's damp, or if fall weather is settling in and the pods are turning brown, harvest whole plants and allow them to dry in a protected place on a sheet or tarp.

Threshing

Threshing is easy if the pods are thoroughly dry.

Yield

These beans are all prolific producers and can yield 4.5 kilograms per 15 metres (10 pounds per 50 feet) of row.

Cooking

For most varieties, an hour's simmering is all that's required and the beans can be used in any of the ways you'd prepare other beans. Adzuki beans are often used in sweet dishes. Limas have a buttery taste and texture while tepary beans have a rich nuttiness. Adzukis are one of the best beans for sprouting.

Saving Seed

The only one to worry about in terms of cross-pollination is limas. Different limas should be separated by as much distance as possible, or you should grow only one cultivar.

Genetically Modified?

No worries here, yet.

Outlook

Adzuki, tepary and lima beans are very promising candidates for the self-sufficient garden wherever summers are long and warm enough to ripen crops.

hot-weather beans

BAKED SOYBEANS

SERVES 4

1 CUP	DRY SOYBEANS, SOAKED	250 ML
2 TBSP	OIL OR BUTTER	30 ML
1	ONION, CHOPPED	1
1	MEDIUM TOMATO, CHOPPED	1
	OR	
1/4 CUP	TOMATO PASTE OR KETCHUP	60 ML
1/4 CUP	MOLASSES	60 ML
1 TBSP	SOY SAUCE	15 ML
1 TSP	DRY MUSTARD	5 ML
1/2 TSP	SEA SALT	2 ML
1/4 TSP	BLACK PEPPER	1 ML

Cook the soybeans and drain, reserving 60 millilitres (1/4 cup) of the cooking liquid. Preheat oven to 180°C (350°F).

Combine beans, liquid and remaining ingredients in a casserole dish and bake, covered, for 30 minutes, then uncovered for 45 minutes.

A couple of finely chopped garlic cloves and/or a chopped green or red pepper are good additions to this casserole. The addition of 125 millilitres (1/2 cup) of corn kernels is another variation.

Soy and Mushroom Salad

Serves 4–6

1 1/2 CUPS	SOYBEANS, SOAKED	375 mL
1 TBSP	OIL	15 mL
1 TBSP	LEMON JUICE	15 mL
1	GARLIC CLOVE, CRUSHED	1
3	CELERY STALKS, CHOPPED	3
3/4 CUP	SLICED MUSHROOMS	180 mL
4	SCALLIONS, FINELY CHOPPED	4
	SALT AND PEPPER TO TASTE	

Cook the beans and drain well. Mix together the oil, lemon juice, garlic, salt and pepper. Toss the beans and vegetables in the dressing. Serve chilled.

MARINATED SOYBEANS

SERVES 4–6

3 CUPS	HOT COOKED SOYBEANS	750 ML
3/4 CUP	OIL	180 ML
1/3 CUP	VINEGAR	80 ML
2	GARLIC CLOVES, FINELY CHOPPED	2
1/2 CUP	SCALLIONS OR CHIVES, CHOPPED	125 ML
1/2 CUP	GREEN OR RED PEPPER, CHOPPED	125 ML
1/3 CUP	CELERY, CHOPPED	80 ML
2 TBSP	FRESH PARSLEY, CHOPPED	30 ML
2 TBSP	FRESH DILL	30 ML
	SALT AND PEPPER TO TASTE	

Place hot beans in a bowl. Combine oil, vinegar, salt, pepper and garlic, then pour over hot beans. Cover and marinate in the refrigerator for several hours.

Stir in scallions, pepper, celery, parsley and dill. Chill again.

Soybean and Rice Curry

Serves 4

3/4 CUP	BROWN RICE, COOKED	180 ML
1 1/2 CUPS	SOYBEANS, COOKED	375 ML
2	MEDIUM ONIONS, CHOPPED	2
3 TBSP	SOY SAUCE	45 ML
2 TBSP	OIL OR BUTTER	30 ML
2 TBSP	NUTRITIONAL YEAST	30 ML
1–2 TSP	CURRY POWDER OR CUMIN	5–10 ML

Sauté onions in butter, mix with soy sauce, yeast and curry powder. Combine rice, beans and sauce. Stir well until heated through.

SOYNUTS

SERVES 2–3

1 CUP	SOYBEANS, COOKED UNTIL JUST TENDER	250 mL
	AND DRAINED	
1/2 CUP	UNSALTED BUTTER	125 mL
1	GARLIC CLOVE, MINCED	1
1 TSP	SALT	5 mL
1 TBSP	SOY SAUCE	15 mL

Preheat onion to 180°C (350°F). Spread soybeans on shallow cookie pan and roast for 30 minutes or until browned, stirring occasionally. Transfer beans to a heatproof bowl.

Meanwhile, over moderate heat, melt butter and cook garlic with salt and soy sauce for three to four minutes. Remove and drizzle with butter mixture. Toss gently to coat. Serve at room temperature.

Soynuts can also be made by skipping the last four ingredients and simply by roasting the beans.

LIMA BEANS DELUXE

SERVES 4

2/3 CUP	DRIED LIMA BEANS, SOAKED	160 ML
2 TBSP	OIL	30 ML
1	LARGE GREEN PEPPER, DICED	1
2	STALKS CELERY, DICED	2
1	ONION, CHOPPED	1
2	GARLIC CLOVES, FINELY CHOPPED	2
1 TSP	SALT	5 ML
1/2 CUP	RAISINS, DRIED CHERRIES OR APPLES	125 ML
1 1/2 TBSP	SESAME SEEDS, TOASTED (OPTIONAL)	25 ML
1 1/2 CUPS	SOUP STOCK (OPTIONAL)	375 ML
1 1/2 CUPS	CHEDDAR CHEESE, GRATED	375 ML

Cook the beans until tender. Drain and reserve the cooking liquid.

Preheat oven to 190°C (375°F). Heat the oil and sauté the green pepper, celery, onion and garlic for 10 minutes or until tender. Combine cooked ingredients with the beans, salt, seeds, fruit and the stock or reserved bean liquid. Mix the ingredients well, then add half the cheese.

Turn the mixture into an oiled one-litre (one-quart) casserole and bake for 25 minutes. Increase oven temperature to 200°C (400°F), top casserole with remaining cheese and bake for 10 to 15 minutes longer to form a crust.

Adzuki or tepary beans can be used instead of limas, and pineapple tidbits could be substituted for the dried fruit.

LIMA OR TEPARY LOAF

SERVES 6

3 CUPS	LIMAS OR TEPARY BEANS, COOKED	750 ML
1 CUP	CELERY, CHOPPED	250 ML
1/4 CUP	ONION, FINELY CHOPPED	60 ML
1 CUP	WHOLE-WHEAT BREAD CRUMBS	250 ML
1/3 CUP	TOMATO SAUCE	80 ML
1 TBSP	SOY SAUCE	15 ML
2 TBSP	SOY OR WHOLE-WHEAT FLOUR	30 ML
1 CUP	NUTS, FINELY CHOPPED	250 ML
	(HAZELNUTS, WALNUTS, ALMONDS)	
1 TSP	DRY SAGE	5 ML
2 TBSP	OIL	30 ML
2 TBSP	PARSLEY, CHOPPED	30 ML
2	EGGS, LIGHTLY BEATEN	2
	SALT TO TASTE	

Preheat oven to 190°C (375°F). Mash the limas or teparies and put in a large bowl. Add all the ingredients and mix well. Turn into a well-oiled loaf pan and bake for 30 minutes until set.

CHAPTER EIGHT

Quinoa and Amaranth

There are so many similarities between quinoa (pronounced keen-wah) and amaranth that it seems appropriate to describe them together. Quinoa, however, is a cool-weather crop and amaranth is a warm-weather one.

Quinoa and amaranth are two very old, high-protein plants that hail from South America. They were held sacred in ancient Inca and Aztec cultures. Both now hold great potential as whole food crops in the Northern Hemisphere. They grow as easily as their weedy relatives (pigweed or lamb's-quarter) and the quality of food they offer far surpasses that of our common grains. Traditional hand-harvesting methods can achieve bounteous harvests.

Quinoa and amaranth are treated as grains although they have broad leaves, unlike the true grains and corn, which are grasses. Their leaves are among the most nutritious of vegetable greens, but it is their fruit that is usually meant when these plants are referred to as "crops." And that fruit or grain is quite special. The protein content of these two foods has an essential amino acid balance that is near the ideal. They both come closer to meeting the genuine protein requirements of the human body than either cow's milk or soybeans. They are high in the amino acid lysine, which is absent in most cereals such as wheat, sorghum, corn and barley.

Both quinoa and amaranth are quite adaptable, disease-free and drought-tolerant plants. They thrive in rich soil as long as it is well drained, but once established both will produce abundant harvests under dry conditions.

The wild relatives of amaranth and quinoa have long been familiar to North American gardeners and are often called by the same name, pigweed. The pigweed that is related to quinoa is also called lamb's-quarter *(Chenopodium album)*, while the ancestor of amaranth is known as red-rooted pigweed or wild amaranth *(Amaranthus retroflexus)*. Both pigweeds have the amazing ability to flower and go to seed at any stage of their growth and both will cross with their cultivated progeny. The grower who wants pure strains of either quinoa or amaranth must therefore pay close attention to weeds.

Most cultivars of amaranth and quinoa grow one to 2.5 metres (four to eight feet) high and, when in flower, are majestic plants with a presence that emits a special radiance in any garden. Quinoa's unique flower hues are most striking up close around dawn or dusk, while amaranth's flamboyant bronze and burgundy tones are dazzling in bright sunshine. Smaller ornamental amaranths such as love-lies-bleeding and prince's-feather have been listed in garden catalogues for hundreds of years.

Soil Preference
Quinoa and amaranth are responsive to nitrogen and phosphorus. Plants grown in

average garden soil will be one to two metres (three to six feet) tall, while those grown in rich soil or compost may reach over 2.5 metres (eight feet). Optimum soil is a well-drained loam, but both plants will do well in all but poorly aerated clay soils.

Varieties

Named varieties of amaranth and quinoa are increasingly available from seed companies. Most North Americans would be hard-pressed to describe the subtle differences in flavour between cultivars. Most black-seeded varieties of amaranth stay quite gritty when cooked, so it is best to use these just for their leaves. All the golden and light-coloured amaranths I've tried are excellent cooked as whole grains and all have delectable greens.

Planting Times

Quinoa grows best where maximum temperatures do not exceed 32°C (90°F) and nighttime temperatures are cool. For most southern Canadian and northern United States sites, the best time to plant quinoa is late April to late June. When soil temperatures are around 15°C (60°F) seedlings emerge within three to four days. However, when quinoa seeds are planted in soil with nighttime temperatures much above that, quinoa, like spinach, may not germinate. In this case, it's best to refrigerate seeds before planting.

Amaranth is a warm-season crop that requires full sun. Best germination occurs when soil temperatures range from 18 to 24°C (65 to 75°F). For southern Canada and the northern United States, this usually means a late-May or early-June planting.

Sowing

The small seeds of amaranth and quinoa will germinate more successfully with a finely prepared surface and adequate moisture. Seeds should be sown no more than a half centimetre (one-quarter inch) deep in rows 45 to 60 centimetres (18 inches to two feet) apart or wide enough to accommodate a rototiller between the rows without damaging the plants. Planting can be done by hand or with a row seeder. Plants should eventually be thinned 15 to 45 centimetres (6 to 18 inches) apart. (Thinnings make great additions to salad.)

One gram (one-third of an ounce) of seed will sow 15 metre (50 feet) of row. A half hectare (one and one-half acre) requires about a half kilogram (one pound) of seed.

Maintenance

Quinoa resembles lamb's-quarter and amaranth resembles red-rooted pigweed, especially in the early stages of growth, so it is best to sow seed in rows to make weeding less confusing. Sowing amaranth cultivars with purple leaves also simplifies weeding. Since the seed is small, you can avoid considerable thinning by mixing it with sand or radish seed before sowing, as is sometimes done with carrots. Amaranth and quinoa are low-maintenance crops but weeds, particularly at the beginning, should be discouraged by cultivation or mulching.

Soil moisture is probably sufficient until early June to germinate the seed. Given good soil moisture, don't water until the plants reach the two- or three-leaf stage. Quinoa and amaranth appear slow-growing at first but both are extremely drought-tolerant and do well on a total of 25 centimetres (10 inches) of water or less. As the plants reach about 30 centimetres (one foot) in height, they start to grow very rapidly, the canopy closes in, weeds are shaded out and less moisture is lost through evaporation.

You may have noticed occasional lamb's-quarter or amaranth weeds succumbing to munching by insect larvae in the flower heads and the same is sometimes true of their cultivated cousins. This won't have any serious impact on the harvest.

Harvesting

Quinoa is ready to harvest when the leaves have fallen, leaving just the dried seed heads. Seeds can be easily stripped upward off the stalk with a gloved hand. Quinoa resists light frosts, especially if the soil is dry. So long as maturing seed is past the green stage, frost will cause little damage and harvesting can be done a day or two later. Extreme hot weather and warm nights inhibit fruit set. It is important to watch the weather when quinoa is ready to be harvested: if rained on, the dry seed can germinate. If the heads are not completely dry, harvest them when you can barely indent the seeds with your thumbnail. They should then be thoroughly dried before storage.

Amaranth keeps on flowering until hit by the first hard frost. Seed will often ripen many weeks before that, usually after about three months. The best way to determine if seed is harvestable is to gently but briskly shake or rub the flower heads between your hands and see if the seeds fall readily. (Numerous small and appreciative birds may give hints as to when to start doing this.)

An easy way to gather ripe grain is, in dry weather, to bend the plants over a bucket and rub the seed heads between your hands. My own preferred threshing method is to rub the flower heads through screening into a wheelbarrow and then to blow away the finer chaff with my air compressor. Cutting and hanging plants to dry indoors does not work very well: the plants become extremely bristly and it is difficult to separate the seed from the chaff.

The best time to harvest amaranth commercially is in dry weather and three to seven days after first frost — a condition not easily met in many places. Most available varieties maintain too high a moisture content to be harvested mechanically before a killing frost.

Clean quinoa and amaranth with screens, by winnowing, with a fan or other blowing device. After harvesting, it is important to further dry your crop to ensure it won't mould in storage. It can be left on trays in the hot sun or placed near an indoor heat source. Stir occasionally until it is as dry as possible. Store seed in airtight containers in a cool, dry place.

Threshing

Unlike beans or true grains, quinoa and amaranth have no hulls to remove. However, quinoa is covered with a bitter substance called saponin, which birds and deer won't touch. Because of this coating, quinoa requires thorough rinsing before cooking. One method is to put the grain in a blender with cool water and at the lowest speed, changing the water until it is no longer soapy. It takes about five water changes to achieve the desired, unfrothy result. Another way is to tie the desired amount of quinoa in a stocking, a loose-weave muslin bag or a pillowcase and run it through a cold-water cycle of an automatic washing machine. You can also get away with less or no rinsing by mixing quinoa with other grains or pulses, rendering the saponin hardly noticeable.

Commercial quinoa has had the saponin removed.

Amaranth has no saponin and no hulls, so can be cooked without additional preparation.

Yield

Thirty to 60 grams (an ounce or two) of seed per plant is common, but you can easily get about 170 grams (six ounces) per plant grown in your best compost. Normal commercial yields for amaranth and quinoa are 500 to 900 kilograms (1200 to 2000 pounds) per half hectare. Agricultural combines are still being adapted to the lightness of the seed, and full harvest potential has yet to be realized. Much better results are obtained from labour-intensive harvesting: yields of more than 2,300 kilograms (5,000 pounds) per half hectare have been reported in Central and South America.

Cooking

Basic recipe: Bring equal volumes of amaranth/quinoa and water to a boil, reduce to a simmer, cover, and cook until all water is absorbed. Amaranth takes about 10 to 12 minutes and quinoa 12 to 15 minutes. For a more porridge-like consistency, use a greater proportion of water. Experiment to find the texture you prefer.

Quinoa and amaranth contain about 16 percent protein, E and B vitamins, calcium, iron and phosphorus. They are easy to digest and have wonderful flavour. Their simple, distinctive taste gives them great versatility for cooking purposes. They can be substituted for other grains in many recipes, though they are much more filling. Because they are not true cereal grains, they can be eaten by people who suffer from cereal-grain allergies.

Young quinoa and amaranth greens make tasty salad material and are high in vitamins (especially calcium and iron), minerals and protein. Carrots juiced with a small amount of either's leaves make a most invigorating drink.

Older greens are wonderful steamed, stir-fried or incorporated into curries or casseroles. Some varieties have better greens than others and are usually so indicated in seed catalogues. One of the tastiest amaranths grown for greens is called tampala. Amaranth is also called Chinese spinach because of its popularity as a green vegetable in China.

Amaranth seed is often ground into flour; it contains more gluten than that of quinoa and combines well with traditional flours in the ratio of one part amaranth to four parts other grains.

Saving Seed

Amaranth and quinoa cross with their wild relatives, so it is important to weed out red-rooted pigweed and lamb's-quarter if you want to maintain pure seed. Amaranth cultivars will cross with each other, as will quinoa cultivars, so grow only one kind of each or separate cultivars by as much distance as you can. Certain varieties, such as purple-leaved amaranth, are easier to sort than others. Lamb's-quarter has a greater branching habit than quinoa and smaller flower heads.

Genetically Modified?

No genetically modified cultivars are in the marketplace.

Outlook

Quinoa and amaranth offer exciting possibilities to growers looking for hardy, easy-to-grow, high-protein foods. They have higher food quality than our common grains such as wheat and oats, and they don't have hulls that need to be removed by machinery prior to cooking. Instructions on most commercial packaging to cook these grains for 30 minutes might be hampering their popularization: 15 minutes' simmering is long enough to provide soft but non-mushy grain. From my own success with growing amaranth and quinoa over many years, I say that the difficulties in cultivating and preparing these two grains are relatively minor and the pleasures obtained in growing and eating them are definitely major.

RECIPES

quínoa

& amaranth

Quinoa or Amaranth Tabbouleh

Serves 4

Tabbouleh, a Middle Eastern salad normally made with bulgur wheat, makes light and refreshing warm-weather fare. Try it with quinoa or amaranth for a delightful new taste.

1 CUP	QUINOA OR AMARANTH	250 ML
1 CUP	PARSLEY, CHOPPED	250 ML
1/2 CUP	SCALLIONS, CHOPPED	125 ML
2 TBSP	FRESH MINT	30 ML
1/2 CUP	LEMON JUICE	125 ML
1/4 CUP	OLIVE OIL	60 ML
2	GARLIC CLOVES, PRESSED	2
1/4 CUP	OLIVES, SLICED	60 ML
	LETTUCE LEAVES, WHOLE	

Simmer quinoa or amaranth in an equal volume of water for 12 to 15 minutes. Allow to cool.

Place all ingredients except lettuce and olives in a mixing bowl and toss together lightly. Chill for an hour or more to allow flavours to blend.

Wash and dry lettuce leaves and use them to line a salad bowl. Add tabbouleh and garnish with olives.

Amaranth or Quinoa and Vegetables

Amaranth and quinoa are dense and much more filling than grains such as rice. A simple yet satisfying meal can be prepared by adding a few tablespoons of chopped and briefly sautéed carrots, scallions or celery to cooked amaranth or quinoa, along with a tablespoon or two of oil or butter.

AMARANTH OR QUINOA PUDDING

SERVES 4

This quick and wholesome dessert is also elegant and tasty. It tastes surprisingly light compared with rice pudding, despite the fact that quinoa is much higher in protein than rice.

2 CUPS	AMARANTH OR QUINOA, COOKED	500 ML
1 CUP	APPLE JUICE	250 ML
1/2 CUP	RAISINS	125 ML
1/2 CUP	ALMONDS, CHOPPED FINE	125 ML
1 1/2 TSP	VANILLA	7 ML
	JUICE OF 1/2 LEMON	
	GRATED RIND OF ONE LEMON	
	DASH OF CINNAMON	

Combine ingredients in a large saucepan, cover and bring to a boil. Reduce heat and simmer for 15 minutes. Pour pudding into individual dessert bowls. Top with a few grapes or strawberries and chill.

AMARANTH OR QUINOA WITH CHOPPED APPLES, RAISINS AND CINNAMON

Stir chopped apples, raisins and cinnamon into cooked amaranth or quinoa. Makes a great hot or cold breakfast cereal.

Amaranth or Quinoa Stir-Fry

Serves 4

2 CUPS	AMARANTH OR QUINOA, COOKED	500 ML
2 TBSP	OIL	30 ML
1	ONION, CHOPPED	1
1	CARROT, SLICED	1
1	CELERY STALK, SLICED	1
1 CUP	MUSHROOMS, SLICED	250 ML
3	GARLIC CLOVES, FINELY CHOPPED	3
1/2 CUP	ALMONDS, CHOPPED	125 ML
1/4 CUP	SUNFLOWER SEEDS	60 ML
2 TBSP	SOY SAUCE	30 ML
1 TSP	SEASONING	5 ML

Sauté veggies, garlic, almonds and seeds in the oil until vegetables are bright in colour and crisp. Add soy sauce, seasonings and amaranth or quinoa. Mix well until warmed through.

Amaranth and Mashed Potatoes

Prepare mashed potatoes in your usual favourite manner. Stir cooked amaranth (about 125 mL [1/2 cup] per three medium potatoes) and cooked onion into hot mashed potatoes. If the amaranth is cooked for only 10 minutes, this makes a great combination of grainy and smooth textures.

CHAPTER NINE

Garlic

G arlic is both a whole food and a whole medicine. For the grower interested in self-reliance, it would be difficult to find an easier, safer, more useful or more potent plant than garlic.

The planting, maintenance and harvest of garlic are always fun and a delight for me. The three or four days in October that are garlic-planting and mulching times are special ones. We pick beautiful weather to put our crop in the freshly tilled ground. Plunking garlic cloves in the earth, then spreading mulch over them, is a very fine way to end the gardening season.

The next thing doesn't come until seven months later when, around mid-April, some weeds start to announce themselves through the mulch. Because of the mulch weeding is easy task and usually doesn't have to be done again. As for watering, it isn't an issue at all because winter and spring rains provide adequate moisture. Well, yes, there's the task of snipping off emerging flower heads in June, but that's certainly not onerous — and we use them with much appreciation in soups, sauces and salads. Nine months after planting, the exciting time of harvesting arrives at the height of summer's glory.

And that's how easy it is to grow garlic. All told, I spend a lot more time watching my garlic grow than trying to make it grow. I've never seen any pests or diseases and my agricultural practices are comprised simply of maintaining soil nutrition and rotating my crops.

Not only has it always been simple for me to grow garlic, it's also been easy me to recommend cultivars to other growers. The fact that all the varieties I grow do well pretty much anywhere in Canada simplifies my garlic catalogue enormously. I don't have to include information about which garlics grow best in Vancouver, Edmonton, Winnipeg, Quebec City or St. John's (as I do for tomatoes, lettuces or broccoli).

Over 1,000 scientific and medically oriented studies have been published on garlic. Garlic improves nutrition, stimulates the immune system, lowers cholesterol, blood pressure and stress and attacks fungi, bacteria and viruses. To me, garlic is simply good food and good medicine. I'm not a garlic fanatic and don't have it with every meal. But I do use it quite regularly and quite liberally. And I do believe that garlic, with its reliable boost to the body's vitality, comes closer than any other plant to being nature's complete medicine chest.

Garlic stories abound. We are told of Egyptian slaves building the pyramids who attributed their vigour to the garlic they ate and refused to work when their ration was reduced. For me, personal anecdotes have supplanted historical or scientific ones. My history includes many hot harvesting days with my brother, Mike, when a clove or two of raw garlic transformed an exhausting task into a lighter one. I've seen garlic applications remove growths on my skin when pharmaceutical antifungal preparations had no effect. And I've had times when I was sure that extra garlic in my diet, particularly in late fall and early winter, saved me from the colds and viruses all around me. Added to this are the dozens of testaments from friends on garlic's wondrous feats. All in all, garlic has convinced me of its powers to heal.

Then there's the alchemy of garlic in the kitchen. Here again I find that, in a very simple way, garlic bestows a unique depth to food. Many dishes taste quite bland without it; garlic enhances most. With the exception of salt, it's by far the most often listed ingredient in recipes around the world. Unlike salt, the threshold at which it becomes "too much" is not precarious. Indeed, it's hard to go wrong with garlic. And there are countless ways to go right.

Varieties

Visitors to Mansell Farm are often amazed at our collection of over 50 varieties of garlic. An oft-repeated comment is, "I thought there was only one kind of garlic." For those who think garlic is garlic, I can say it is simply not so. Garlic varieties differ in size, shape and colour; they differ in strength, pungency and texture. As for taste, my garlic cohorts and I are having a great time creating a vocabulary suited to the subtle but notable distinctions among them.

Most strains have come to me with names of countries attached, such as Russian, French, Italian or Spanish. Some strains are named after people, as in Purple Max. And one variety of unknown origin, which has been been grown here on Salt Spring Island for 30 years, I've come to call Salt Spring garlic.

The commercial garlic best known to consumers has small cloves clustered piggyback-style in concentric layers with no central stalk; this kind of garlic is often referred to as a "nonbolting" or "soft-necked" garlic. By contrast, rocambole garlics are "hard-necked," with cloves placed adjacent to each other around a thick central stalk. Rocamboles are a pleasure to use because their cloves are very large and easy to peel.

Elephant garlic is not a true garlic but a member of the leek family. It is in demand because of its size and excellent storage quality. It's not as robust in flavour as regular garlic and has a characteristic bitterness, although it is good for baking. Some regular garlics certainly grow as large as elephant garlic.

Soil Preference

Garlic prefers a sunny location and will do well in many types of soil. However, like its cousin the onion, it appreciates rich, well-drained, sandy loam with plenty of humus. For poor and acidic (below pH 5.5) soil, you'd do well to dig in compost or aged manure along with wood ash, dolomite lime or crushed oyster shells. A caution, however, against too rich a soil, which may cause the tops to overdevelop. I've found that soils that are only moderately fertile yield the finest garlics.

You may know that garlic repels some pests. For this reason it is often recommended as a companion for roses, tomatoes and cabbages — something you might consider when choosing its location in your garden.

Planting Time

The best time to plant garlic is between August and December, though I most often recommend late September or October. Planting any time in this period will give the plants the earliest possible start in spring and result in a harvest of large bulbs the following summer. Garlic puts down an extensive root system in the fall and winter, then sprouts green growth in early spring. Spring sowings work, but they give the plants less chance to size up before shorter days trigger bulbs to form. Garlic needs a minimum of 100 days to mature.

Planting in the fall will help make garlic the carefree crop that it can be. Moisture in the soil is generally enough for the entire growing period, and one rarely has to water garlic unless May or June are unusually dry. The fall headstart ensures garlic will stay ahead of the weeds in spring.

Sowing

Garlic can be planted in single or double rows or in intensive beds with five or six plants across. To begin, break apart the bulbs without peeling any of the skin. Plant individual cloves, wide part down, about five centimetres (two inches) deep so that the pointed end is slightly below the soil surface. I usually leave 10 or 12 centimetres (four or five inches) between plants but cloves can be planted even more closely in rich soil.

Maintenance

A mulch will encourage root growth in winter. In cold climates, snow serves as a mulch. Mulching material such as straw or grass clippings will also slow weed growth in the spring. Repeated applications of mulch will minimize weeding as well as keep the soil moist and friable. If possible, avoid mulching with hay containing viable seed: garlic does not appreciate competing with weeds for light and nourishment.

When weeding, practise shallow cultivation to avoid disturbing garlic roots near the soil surface.

Other than weeding, garlic needs little care once it's planted. An occasional dose of fish fertilizer or seaweed solution will boost leaf and bulb growth. Because most growth occurs before the summer sun starts to dry out the soil, garlic normally doesn't require much irrigation. To allow for optimum underground bulb curing, avoid watering for a few weeks before harvest, which is usually around the end of July. If flower heads form at any time (usually in June), cut them right back so that the plants put all their energy into bulb growth rather than seed formation.

If garlic does flower, the bulbils that may later form in clusters at the top of the stalk can be used as an alternative way of multiplying your crop. (A few varieties have bulbils that form partway up the stem.) Bulbils planted in the fall of one year develop small, undivided bulbs or bulbs of tiny cloves by the next fall. These must be dug and replanted to produce full-size bulbs in the following year.

Harvesting and Storage

Most garlics grow about waist-high and come to maturity toward the end of July or in early August. However, plants started from store-bought garlic may mature as late as September in the first year. The best time to harvest garlic is when at least half to 80 percent of the foliage has turned yellow. For braiding, it's best to harvest when stalks are still half green. Stalks of some varieties will fall over when mature.

If mulched well, plants can be pulled easily by hand. Otherwise, dig them up carefully to avoid puncturing. Sometimes a fork plunged into the soil near but not against the plant is all that's needed to loosen for pulling.

Some sources recommend curing garlic in the sun for two days to two weeks, bringing it in or covering it if dew or rain is expected. I used to leave my harvest outside for several days, always with success. But given the atmospheric changes of recent years, and hearing stories of friends' garlic frying in the sun on excessively hot summer days, has made me wary. I now hang my fresh-pulled garlic to cure in the large loft of our barn. Bulbs curing with insufficient airflow may mildew as their moisture leaves them, and individual cloves exposed to the sun may turn green.

After curing for 10 days to two weeks, the dirty outer skins of the bulbs and lower stalk will slip off easily. The cloves on good bulbs will still be held together neatly by a white, purplish, bronze or brownish paper-thin skin. Remove the dirt gently, but leave as much skin as possible intact. The roots can be twisted off or cut at this point. Garlic plants with pliant stalks can be now braided or hung in bunches. Alternatively, cut the bulbs off the stalk, leaving 2.5 centimetres (one inch) of the top to facilitate later clove separation. These can be hung in mesh bags. Whatever the method, garlic should be kept in a cool, airy room for optimum storage.

Save the biggest cloves from your biggest bulbs for planting, which you can do almost at once. The rest are ready to eat. For a month or two they are milder and sweeter than when they've cured a while, providing special delight in the middle of summer. Use bruised, punctured, exposed or otherwise suspect cloves first. Don't store your bulbs in a refrigerator as the cold causes cloves to sprout, changing their flavour and texture. We keep our house garlic in open baskets in a cool room. The cloves you save for eating will last almost until the next summer's crop. Smaller, less oily varieties will last longest. While you wait for the year's harvest, you can enjoy garlic leaves, flowering tops and the bulbils that form within the flower. They are excellent, though relatively unknown. They can be used fresh, refrigerated for long periods, or frozen, and cooked in many of the ways you'd use the cloves themselves.

Yield

Each clove you plant ends up being a bulb, so a variety will multiply by the average number of cloves per bulb. Bulbs of rocambole varieties often weigh more than 85 grams (three ounces), so a 7.5-metre (25-foot) row of garlic can easily yield six kilograms (14 pounds) of garlic.

Genetically Modified?

There are no genetically modified garlic varieties in the stores. However, a lot of commercial garlic has been irradiated as well as treated with sprout inhibitors and fungicides.

Outlook

To anyone who appreciates garlic, whether for cooking or medicine, the taste and texture of homegrown or local garlic is noticeably superior than what's available commercially. Given that garlic is one of the easiest garden crops to grow, it is likely that the current rise in popularity of homegrown garlic will continue.

RECIPES

garlic

ALISON'S CELESTO PESTO

MAKES 4 CUPS

16–22	GARLIC CLOVES	16–22
1	MEDIUM ONION, QUARTERED	1
1 1/2 CUP	WALNUTS, ALMONDS, SUNFLOWER SEEDS	375 ML
	OR COMBINATION OF THESE	
1 CUP	EXTRA-VIRGIN OLIVE OIL (OR MORE)	250 ML
8 CUPS	BASIL LEAVES, LOOSELY PACKED	2 L
1 1/2 CUPS	CURLY PARSLEY LEAVES	375 ML
1 CUP	PARMESAN CHEESE, GRATED	250 ML
	SALT TO TASTE	

Place garlic and onion in bowl of food processor and chop finely. Add nuts/or seeds and process to a smooth paste. When using almonds or sunflower seeds, it may be necessary to add a little oil at this stage.

Put in basil leaves to fill bowl. Close lid, engage motor and drizzle oil into bowl to encourage the basil to break down.

Add parsley leaves and cheese and continue to process, adding oil as necessary.

Add remaining basil and salt and process with oil until desired consistency is reached. This pesto is intended to be quite thick, but oil or cream will thin it nicely.

Garlic Soup

2	GARLIC BULBS, SEPARATED INTO CLOVES,	2
	PEELED AND CHOPPED	
1	LARGE ONION, MINCED	1
3 TBSP	OLIVE OIL	45 ML
2 TSP	FRESH BASIL, MINCED	10 ML
1/2 TSP	FRESH TARRAGON, MINCED	2 ML
4 CUPS	FRESH TOMATOES, PEELED AND CHOPPED	1 L
4 CUPS	VEGETABLE BROTH OR WATER	1 L
	SALT AND FRESHLY GROUND	
	BLACK PEPPER TO TASTE	

Sauté garlic and onion in oil in a soup pot over medium heat, being careful not to brown them. When they are translucent, add the chopped tomato, basil and tarragon, then stir for two minutes. Add the liquid, bring to a boil, then reduce to a simmer. Cook for about 45 minutes. Add salt and pepper if needed.

This soup can be made more substantial by adding cooked grain or pasta just before serving.

BAKED GARLIC

Slow baking makes garlic quite mild, fragrant and nutty-sweet. It can be used by itself or to enhance grilled foods, pizzas, focaccia breads and pastas.

The softened parts of each clove can be squeezed from the skin onto buttered bread and the bread can be dipped into the sauce. The addition of cream cheese to the bread makes for a real gourmet treat.

1–2	GARLIC BULBS PER PERSON	1–2
1/4 CUP	BUTTER	60 ML
1/4 CUP	OLIVE OIL	60 ML
1/2 TSP	FRESH THYME, MINCED	2 ML

Preheat oven to 150°C (300°F). Remove the papery outer skin from the garlic but leave cloves intact around their central stalk. Place the bulbs in a small baking dish that will just contain them. Melt the butter with the olive oil and thyme. Brush the garlic bulbs generously with the mixture. Cover and bake for about an hour, basting occasionally until the cloves are tender. Remove cover and bake for 20 more minutes. Remove the garlic heads from the baking dish and whisk a little water into the baking juices to make a light sauce. Pour the sauce over the baked garlic and serve. Garnish with sprigs of parsley and thyme if desired.

GARLIC GREENS BUTTER

Fresh garlic greens can be used similarly to chives or green onions. As well, the flower tops and their stems are a special treat in June and July and make an unusual and special addition to stir-fries. (Yes, it's normal procedure to cut off emerging flower heads so that garlic plants put all their energy into bulb formation.)

1/3 CUP	BUTTER, SLIGHTLY SOFTENED	80 ML
1–2 TBSP	GARLIC GREENS, MINCED	15–30 ML
2 DROPS	WORCESTERSHIRE SAUCE	2 DROPS
2 DROPS	HOT PEPPER SAUCE	2 DROPS
1/4 TSP	DIJON MUSTARD	1 ML

Mash together all ingredients in a small bowl. Taste; add more seasonings for spicier butter.

TANYA'S DRAGON SLAYER

This recipe uses the curly tops of the ripening garlic plant as a substitute for or complement to pasta. June is when you'll find these flowers in your garden.

Snip off garlic tops and carefully slice them lengthwise in four.

Steam them until they soften (seven to 10 minutes) and add them to your favourite noodles and sauce.

The real "dragon slayer" is to serve them by themselves, topped by your most potent garlic pesto!

GARLIC TOAST WITH KAMUT SPROUTS

2	SLICES OF YOUR FAVOURITE BREAD	2
2 TBSP	GARLIC CHOPPED, FINELY	30 ML
2 TBSP	FLAX OIL, BUTTER OR MARGARINE	30 ML
1/4 CUP	KAMUT BERRIES, JUST STARTING TO SPROUT (OR OTHER WHEAT OR HULLESS BARLEY)	60 ML

Pour the flax oil evenly over the toasted bread. Sprinkle the garlic evenly as well, then the kamut sprouts. A layer of seed or nut butter spread over the toast before covering with sprouts makes for an even more delectable mixture of flavours and textures.

A note on sprouting:
Soak grains overnight in twice their volume of water. Drain. Rinse and drain two or three times a day until the sprouts are one-half to one centimetre (one-quarter to one-half inch) long. One cup of dried grains will become two cups sprouted in about three days. Sprouted grains become remarkably sweet and pleasantly chewy.

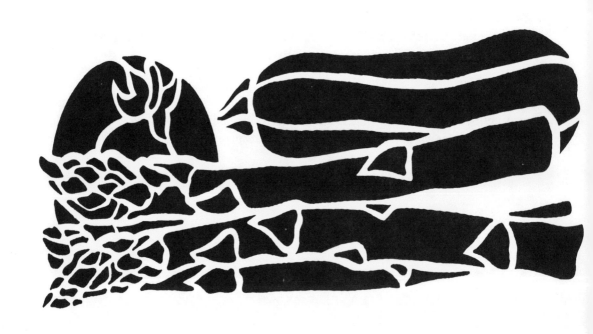

The Whole and Organic Foods Community

The simple act of saving seeds has lately become an extremely important one. Unprecedented changes are going on in the world of seeds that threaten the very safety of the food we eat. Corporate mergers of seed growers have accelerated at such a pace that there are now only a few giant rulers. Patented seeds have become common in catalogues. Millions of hectares of farmland are being planted with bio-engineered seeds.

Certain transnational corporations have openly declared their intention of gaining total control of the world's food supply. As things now stand they are not far from so doing. Farmers are being taken to court for saving seed. Plants that have always belonged to everyone are now "owned" by corporations. It has become almost impossible to find food products in North America that are not derived from genetically modified seeds.

The simple, savable seeds that are part of 10,000 years of agricultural tradition are threatened with extinction. There is everything right with these seeds and they are all we need to grow healthy food. If we don't continue to use them we will lose them forever.

The pollution of seeds, our forever friends, represents to more and more people the very last straw. You can't find pure water any more, can't breathe clean air, and now our daily meals are being contaminated beyond belief. The practice of tinkering with genes from totally different species and mixing them up in our food, with no testing, no consultation and no notification, is bringing people to the view that corporations are out of control. Genetically altered foods are being foisted on us by so-called life sciences companies in the name of health, safety and humanitarianism while in reality they are an experiment with potentially deadly consequences.

Terminator seeds are part of the arsenal of these same corporations that are promising us hope for the future. They more transparently reveal the name of the game to be profit and control. Such seeds especially threaten the livelihoods of "Third World" farmers (usually women) who have traditionally saved their own seed. That minds would design seeds to terminate themselves is incomprehensible to most people. A perusal of the histories of some of these same transnational corporations is quite scary: they are manufacturers of the most virulent poisons used in warfare.

The issue of seeds has the potential to be a very big wake-up call. The confused mindset that blasts foreign genes into seeds, that patents seeds, that kills seeds, is clearly one that would destroy the very garden that feeds us.

Seeds remind us, if we but hold them in our hands, that we are a lot bigger than our current preoccupations. Wheat and barley, soybeans and sesame seeds got here because countless other people held them in their hands. They got here in a dance of people and earth that will only go on if both partners are honoured. They got here not by diminishing life but by letting life flourish.

We got here the same way. We got here because life keeps producing more diverse and divine expressions of herself, not reducing herself to sameness and certainty.

An agriculture that becomes a monoculture cannot work for very long. In North America, it worked for the second half of the 20th century because there was a deep bank of soil for starters, plus trees to hold water and stabilize the weather. Now trees are gone, soil has eroded, wells are empty and the weather is predictable only in its unpredictability.

The transnational corporations that are cramming their gene-altered crops down our throats are doing so with the same arrogance and ignorance they've shown during the past 50 years of industrial agriculture. Creating transgenic crops is an extreme extension of the belief that we can totally control nature and get away with it. But the writing on the wall has become more and more underlined for anyone who looks at the current state of our environment. It has quickly become obvious that genetically manipulating crops is the same bad science as breeding crops that grow well only with the constant application of chemicals.

Already 90 percent of biotech firms have gone bankrupt. Most major bioengineered crops have bombed, too, including transgenic tomatoes, cotton and potatoes. And genetically modified foods have been rejected in Europe, where people have more Earth-connected traditions of healthy food.

The largest corporations remain, and have so much money that they can say and do anything. Will we soon have only the corporate-created food that some chief executive officers are promising? And if that time comes, how much will that food cost us?

Who is saying what we can do instead? We don't have a high proportion of people in North America who really care about their food. Most people don't even know where their food comes from or how it is produced. We don't have many farmers in North America who truly know that diversity works far better than monoculture. We don't even have many farmers left who know that you can't farm from the top floor of a corporate office tower.

Can we stop buying into processes and products that are designed only to make money, before stopping becomes impossible? Fortunately, everything is changing as fast as today's weather. New ways of looking at things are starting to make sense. Why should food be so wrapped up by money? There is already a vast surplus of whole grains and beans being grown in North America. Why shouldn't food be a right, instead of a privilege? Couldn't we all be well fed?

Why not encourage people to have a rewarding livelihood by farming the richness of the earth? To live on the land and derive satisfaction and fulfillment from the infinite beauty and entertainment of nature? Why shouldn't we all spread out a bit, instead of choking in the cities, and start to realize, as well, the vast potential for growing food within our urban environments?

What about the most radical idea of all that's starting to germinate? The Earth is pretty messed up these days, but it's still likely the most incredible place in the universe. Why should the tiniest proportion of people have all the power and resources? Why don't we go for it and try to use all our smarts for mutual benefit? Why don't we create a place where all life is honoured and cherished?

Seeds are perhaps the most potent beginning point we've got right now. They have the power to feed, clothe and shelter us. They have the power to clean our air and water. The threat of their extermination must rally us to their protection, preservation, multiplication and enhancement. For seeds to remain public treasure, we must embrace them and create agendas for them that are people-oriented rather than power-oriented.

The great news is, and we hope you will soon agree, that normal seeds are easy and fun to save. Our remaining stock of open-pollinated seeds can be perpetuated without any special knowledge, equipment or resources. This section is about how to do so and how to do it with other people. By becoming responsible for seed saving instead of depending on governments or seed companies, we can help save ourselves. When the powers that be bite the dust, we will be sustaining the good Earth.

CHAPTER TEN

Hybrid, Patented and Biotech Seeds versus Organic and Public Seeds

A round the world a serious situation is threatening the safety of our food supply. While many people ponder the consequences of global warring and global warming, perhaps the largest planetary catastrophe is unfolding in the garden. Varieties of food plants that have been grown for generations are being replaced by technologically manufactured ones. Reducing the diversity of life narrows our options for an already uncertain future, when it will be essential that our food crops have resistance to pests and diseases as well as the ability to adapt to climate changes, fluctuating water supplies, holes in the ozone and acid rain. To simplify the environment as is being done with agriculture is to destroy the complex interrelationships by which the natural world is held together. Responsibility for restoring food variety and abundance may well rest in the hands of home-garden seed savers: hands that still touch and work the earth.

Salt Spring Seeds

Being the owner of a seed company has given me a unique perspective on the world of food, but there certainly wasn't much preparation in my background in terms of studies in biology or agriculture. I grew up in the suburbs of Montreal with no exposure to vegetable gardens. When I went to McGill University, I majored in anthropology.

On the other hand, something in me was doing some major preparation. Where the urge came from I don't know, but I pestered my parents for many years until finally they allowed me to grow a tiny garden under a back stairway.

Strange but true, four years after I had graduated and moved to British Columbia I wrote a best-selling book on edible and medicinal wild plants. As soon as I stopped moving around, I was turning over soil and trying to grow as many different things as I could.

When I started experiencing the delights of beans, soybeans and quinoa, I found myself wanting to reveal the goodness of these crops to others. The beauty of their harvests was the seeds themselves. I could give people seeds not only to cook but to plant as well. I encouraged them to save seed from their own plantings. Little did I know that this would lead to the development of my own seed company.

I was especially enthused by the Black Jet soybeans I had been growing successfully. Despite what I had read about soybeans, this variety matured in the cool summers of the Gulf Islands, was easy to digest and tasted wonderful. When my enthusiasm was confirmed by many people to whom I mailed seeds across British Columbia, the thought came that I should keep doing it. My first catalogue, in 1986, listed six beans: quinoa and the Black Jets. I thought I was onto something most special: great foods we could easily grow but didn't.

There were many surprises. They included special and little-known varieties of favas, garbanzos, dry peas, amaranth, barley, wheat and oats. My message came to be that we could have an exciting, satisfying, healthy and inexpensive diet with whole beans and grains as the main components. I couldn't understand why other seed catalogues didn't feature these crops. They were so easy and rewarding to grow. And my customers thought so, too.

Alongside the crops exploration was the desirability of organic growing methods over chemical ones, and open-pollinated seeds over hybrids.

Hybrid Seeds

Hybrid seeds, in simple terms, are seeds from selected mixed parentage in which the breeders control the lines. Seed from hybrid plants doesn't come true, so you have to purchase new seed annually from the seed company.

Hybrid versus open-pollinated wasn't that big an issue for me in the early days of Salt Spring Seeds, because there were still a lot of non-hybrid seeds in catalogues then. And I must admit that I was somewhat convinced by all the "high performance" hype about hybrid seeds.

A trip to Ethiopia in 1993 educated me as to the truth about hybrid seeds. Hybrid seeds should more rightly be called "high response" seeds. They perform well if grown with chemical fertilizers, herbicides, pesticides and lots of water. But many open-pollinated varieties have more flavour, are hardier and have more flexibility than hybrids. They taste better because breeders can't manipulate the complex quality of flavour, the way they can size or shape. They grow well without high inputs because they have been selected under conditions free of such artifice. In the case of hybrids, what destroys one plant has the potential to destroy them all, whereas the diversity inherent in open-pollinated varieties allows some of them to survive even if disease strikes.

The bottom line with hybrid seeds is that they exist to make money for their owners. So it is understandable that most catalogues these days promote expensive hybrids.

Patented Seeds

It took rather a long time for petrochemical and pharmaceutical corporations to realize that huge profits could be made by linking seeds with their other products. Until recently, there was an unspoken assumption in North America that seeds were a public rather than a private resource. The maintenance of food security and the development of safe and nutritious crops was considered an important responsibility of government. In the 1990s, however, cost-cutting governments were only too happy to let transnational corporations come on fast and furious in taking over the agricultural sector.

One sinister result of corporate seed investment has been the appearance of more and more patented seeds. It is illegal for anyone to sell these seeds except their "owners." In some cases it is even illegal to save them. Patented seeds aren't necessarily hybrids; they can also be open-pollinated seeds with minor modifications. No matter that the bulk of the work of selecting and growing out these seeds has taken place over hundreds of years. No matter that the work was done by thousands of farmers and gardeners who understood that seeds belong to the Earth.

The seed industry has become increasingly consolidated to the point that there are now only a handful of main players. These agrichemical companies would have us believe that our food needs can best be met by high energy-input production technologies. Most commercial seed companies have become seed merchants rather than seed growers and buy their seeds from these few sources. Seed companies like my own, that actually grow their seeds and that feature hardy, open-pollinated and regionally adapted seed varieties, have become a rarity.

The Ethiopians revealed to me more than the truth about hybrids. They showed me a very serious and sophisticated approach to seed saving. There, plant diversity is equated with food security. Farmers and gene-bank scientists have high respect for each other. Databases are extensive and strong back-up systems are in place.

When I returned to Canada, I naively imagined I might work with the Canadian Department of Agriculture both in my capacity as owner of a seed company and as a director of the Heritage Seed Program of Canada (now called Seeds of Diversity). I didn't know that the writing was already on the wall and that the federal government was retiring from basic seed research and preservation. The termination, in the mid-1990s, of some of the agriculture stations across the country as well as the closure of Canada's two most important gene banks in Ottawa and Smithfield, Ontario, were a wake-up call for me.

The Cost of Corporate Seeds
Now that huge companies control the development, production and distribution of seeds, the high cost of this control is becoming only too evident worldwide. Corporate

standards impose uniform agricultural strategies on diverse situations. Corporate control of agriculture alienates farmers and gardeners globally from traditional, sustainable food production methods and radically alters the quality of both seeds and food.

Plant breeders in these companies develop new varieties for purely economic reasons: uniformity, ease of transportation and shelf life. These varieties are also created to depend on high levels of fertilizers, to tolerate high levels of pesticides and to survive herbicides. The obvious reason for this is that the companies themselves manufacture these products. Qualities such as flavour and nutritional content have been sacrificed. Not only are input costs higher, but there are also greater health risks for farmers and an increased burden of toxic chemicals in our food and in our environment.

The escalation of dependency on these same transnational corporations is staggering. Farmers worldwide have been bedazzled by new hybrid wonder seeds for a few seasons, only to find that the resulting plants require increasingly greater fertilizer and pesticide inputs at correspondingly inflated prices. At the same time, heirlooms that represent hundreds and thousands of years of local adaptation have not been planted and have either been consumed or lost their viability. Priceless genetic heritage has disappeared. As well, the soil has begun to deteriorate, pests to increase, yields to decrease, and it has become apparent that the hybrids not only taste inferior but also are not suited to local growing conditions. No longer able to afford the costs associated with hybrid seeds, let alone the costs of growing their traditional crops, small-scale farmers, especially those in Third World countries, bear greater and greater debt to become virtual slaves of the multinational companies.

Yes, the largest seed companies are also the largest producers of fungicides, herbicides, insecticides and chemical fertilizers. Despite the 1990s swing toward research and development of environmentally friendly products, this is not likely to happen within the seed industry: there is little profit to be made in popularizing a diverse range of pest-resistant, open-pollinated crops.

Technological breeding is also displacing the very resource — that is, the range of plant varieties — upon which the technology is based. The world food system now depends on very few plant varieties: 95 percent of human nutrition is derived from no more than 30 plants, and their genetic vulnerability is extreme. For example, two varieties of peas account for 96 percent of North American consumption of this vegetable; for dry beans, two varieties account for 60 percent; and for millet, only three varieties exist. Of global cereal nutrition, 75 percent is provided by three crops — wheat, rice and maize. Since 1900, over 86 percent of known apple varieties have become extinct. Since 1900, 2,300 pear varieties have become extinct.

In North America nearly 4,000 commercial varieties of standard, open-pollinated vegetables are endangered because seed companies no longer carry them. Plant-patenting legislation in Europe has already resulted in the extinction of over half of all European vegetable varieties. At the rate plant varieties are currently being lost, our repasts will soon become exceedingly limited.

And now we have genetically modified seeds entering the marketplace. GMO seeds, also called transgenic, bioengineered or biotech seeds, have raised the stakes to levels unimaginable a few years ago. In 1994, I was on a committee trying to make sure risks were evaluated before such seeds would be allowed to be tested. But by 1998 it was clear that public input was (and still is) ignored. Governments have allowed the transnationals themselves to evaluate the risks of their engineered seeds. Now test sites have given way to massive plantations. In 1994 there was virtually no acreage planted to biotech crops; less than a decade later, a handful of agrochemical corporations are now in the process of totally dominating global food production with genetically engineered food.

Genetically Modified Seeds

GMO seeds contain genetic material, DNA, from foreign organisms such as fish, bacteria, animals or other plants. The DNA is engineered into the seed to generate a specific trait that would not normally occur. Tomatoes have been given genes from flounder, a cold-water fish, so they can survive in freezing cold weather. Other vegetables have been gene-spliced to make them ripen more slowly or quickly, according to market demand. Some plants are designed to produce their own pesticides.

Nearly 3,000 varieties of plants, animals and bacteria have already been altered genetically in North America. Most bioengineered crops have been produced to withstand applications of their corporation's leading brands of herbicides.

As in the past, with the so-called miracle seeds of the so-called green revolution, there are all-knowing assertions from the corporations that genetically modified seeds are environmentally friendly and will lead to health benefits, an end to world hunger and reduced use of pesticides and herbicides. As in the past, the truth is the exact opposite. Only this time, the level of exploitation is much more scary.

No one knows the long-range implications of biotechnology and no one is doing any long-range testing.

The techniques for inserting DNA fragments are imprecise and unpredictable. Scientists don't claim to understand how gene tinkering affects the host plant and there have already been unexpected mutations that have created new and higher levels of toxins in foods (for example, a genetically engineered form of the food supplement tryptophan that produced lethal contaminants).

The effect of eating GMO foods is unknown, but there is already clear evidence that genetic engineering can produce serious allergic reactions. Researchers tested a GMO soybean with an added Brazil nut gene (to boost protein content); people with a sensitivity to Brazil nuts, who had no adverse reaction to non-GMO soybeans, showed allergic reactions. In 1999, allergic reactions to soyfoods increased by 50 percent. Could this have something to do with a similar increase in GMO soybean production? Even the cosmetic appearance for which some crops have been designed can be dangerously misleading: a bright red tomato could be many weeks old and of little nutritional value.

Releasing seeds with modified genes into the environment has some obvious dangers. Transferred genes can escape through cross-pollination into wild species or other non-engineered crops. Newly acquired genes may cause plants to become weed problems, accelerate insect resistance or result in new types of viruses. Gene scientists have been saying that such things could never happen, but some significant events have already proved them wrong.

Several corporations have spliced genes of the soil bacterium *Bacillus thuringensis*, also known as Bt, into food crops. For many years, organic growers have used Bt selectively as a relatively safe and quite effective pesticide. In 1997, some bugs became immune to Bt for the first time through extended exposure and accelerated adaptation to it. Also, it has been found that Bt toxin in residues of GMO corn and rice persists in soils for up to eight months and depresses natural microbial activity.

Research projects in the United States have confirmed that when monarch butterfly caterpillars feed on milkweed contaminated by the pollen from GMO corn, they die. European studies have found the same problems in ladybugs and green lacewings, both beneficial insects. It has been reported that honeybees may be harmed by feeding on GMO canola, and GMO pollen has been detected in honey near GMO canola sites.

Early in 2000, word came out that some weeds in Alberta had become resistant to three kinds of herbicides. They had picked up genes from three different genetically modified varieties of the rapeseed crop, canola.

And as for the supposed health benefits of GMO foods, I've been hearing that story for more than 10 years. In the early 1990s, I started receiving a publication put out by a group in the United States called the Union of Concerned Scientists, in which all GMO research in food crops was monitored. A decade later, I have yet to see a single corporate GMO experiment with nutrition in mind.

Biotech engineers label protests against their seeds as "unscientific," but in reality what these scientists are asking us to treat as holy is something that at this stage is still a clumsy, hit-or-miss technology. Even on their own terms, GMO scientists have already seen many notable transgenic crop failures, including GMO tomatoes, potatoes and cotton; many farmers have lost millions of dollars because crops didn't perform as predicted. Yet billions are still being invested in biotech seeds.

As for claims of reduction of pesticides and herbicides, the facts are glaringly obvious. The creation by genetic engineers of crops that produce their own pesticides results in a persistent concentration of pesticides over vast acreages.

The promotion of herbicide-resistant crops allows the farmer to use more herbicide: Roundup Ready crops mean more sales of Roundup.

It is understandable why biotech corporations downplay the hazards of GMO seeds: the narrowing of biodiversity and the possibility of long-term, irreversible disruption of ecosystems would be profitable for them. The results would be continued and increased reliance on chemical inputs for agriculture, as well as increased reliance on biotech solutions to agricultural problems.

And in what ways will foods with modified genes modify us, the humans who eat them? "Not to worry," say the gene splicers. "We know best what's good for you — and, by the way, you don't have any choice."

Heritage Seeds

Farmers worldwide have provided food for over 10,000 years by annually saving and selecting seed from their crops. Now, for the first time, seeds have owners and they come with rules and regulations that exclude farmers and gardeners from the seed-saving process. (When you grow biotech seeds, you sign a contract to sow only those seeds, use only the corporation's products, allow inspections at any time and not save seeds.) Many gardeners lament the loss of countless favourite varieties that were suited to the home garden but didn't measure up economically because they were irregularly shaped, weren't the accepted colour, thrived only in certain soils or couldn't stand up to shipping conditions.

Heirloom or heritage varieties are those that over time and in given regions out-perform others for any number of reasons. It is usually accepted that 50 years of high performance is long enough to merit the "heirloom" tag. These traditional, open-polli-nated seeds have disappeared as local seed companies have been bought out and farm families stop farming.

Some concerned people have responded to the certainty of yet more erosion of genetic diversity by establishing thriving seed savers' exchanges. Seeds of Diversity Canada and Seed Savers Exchange in the U.S., whose addresses appear at the end of this book, are inspiring projects about which anyone interested in saving seeds should know. These networks are dedicated to searching out and preserving endangered food crops as well as those varieties from older farmers that are considered heirlooms. They enable members to share wonderful and precious varieties of plants that would other-wise be unavailable. Through their publications, members learn not only about seed saving and genetic preservation but also about heritage gardens, seed companies that stock heirloom varieties and the backgrounds of cultivars that are part of our heritage. Seeds of Diversity and Seed Savers Exchange are essentially living gene banks, actively addressing a situation that threatens the safety and survival of food as we've known it.

Organic Seeds

Seed savers exchanges have a very significant role, but it is important to remember that it is not only our seed heritage that is endangered but our entire agricultural heritage. Farmers are also becoming extinct. Fortunately, the organic movement came on strong throughout the 1990s. More and more people are appalled by the devastation caused by the short-term, profit-driven strategies of corporate agribusiness and want to enjoy and support a safe, alternative food supply. Organic has come to mean Earth-friendly agricultural practices that enhance the soil, not deplete or poison it. It means farmworker health. It means social justice. It means the surrounding communities of people, plants and animals are not subject to toxic pollution. It encourages citizens everywhere to recognize a partnership with the farmers and retailers who they know are committed to providing wholesome food.

The organic production and distribution community, now encompassing a multitude of small- to moderate-size enterprises, has prospered because people have been willing to purchase food at prices more in line with the true costs of producing it. Ten years ago, organic growing was still mostly dismissed as being idealistic and impractical. Now, it has been shown beyond any doubt to enhance everyone's health and well-being.

But chemical and biotech corporations and giant supermarket chains want to take over organic interests, too. They would like to see new regulations to standardize the definition of organic food. These regulations would weaken organic standards considerably and would allow, for example, biotech seeds to be called "organic." On top of this, the desired regulations would prohibit organic producers from upholding and promoting their own stricter standards. An American initiative to institute such changes was temporarily blocked in the spring of 1998: rapid internet communication resulted in hundreds of thousands of protests. As things stand, however, genetically modified foods still do not require labelling as such in the marketplace; nor do genetically modified seeds.

The latest agribusiness creation takes techno-wizardry to unprecedented rudeness: the so-called terminator seed is designed to sabotage its own germination. As if hybrid, patented and GMO seeds as well as corporate legal prohibitions against seed-saving weren't already enough assertion of seed ownership!

Simple, Savable Seeds

Growing all the seeds for Salt Spring Seeds has indeed given me a unique perspective on the world of food. I can say with certainty that we don't really need technological-ly produced designer seeds. The ones that have been lovingly handed on to us by our forebears, imbued with their dedicated love of the land, work far better than those imbued with greed for profit, power and control.

To my mind, the concept of "owning" a seed represents an extreme example of human entrenchment in maintaining power over others and power over nature. To say that everything in the world is private property, waiting to be discovered and pos-sessed, sadly reflects our alienation from the natural world. The pervasiveness of such a myopic outlook places the onus on home-garden seed savers to rediscover, popularize and preserve the superb food varieties that still exist, albeit tenuously, as everyone's heritage.

Growing all the seed for my seed company has opened my eyes to the perfection already inherent in the genetic code of a vegetable seed. I know that this perfection is only realized through the seed's interaction with all the aspects of a particular environment — of which the gardener is a major element. The seeds from plants I have grown over the longest time have the greatest vitality and vibrancy, a power that I believe has come from our mutual adaptation as they become part of a unique microclimate under my guardianship. Plants from seed I send out across the continent may be robust, but I know they can become more so when gardeners enter into an enduring relationship with them that allows their growing to be co-creative.

Saving our own seed restores agricultural creativity and genius to what it has been until recent times. Saving seed fosters sustainability by fulfilling a basic need at home, instead of relying on seed companies or governments.

CHAPTER ELEVEN

Saving Seeds

This chapter details seed-saving procedures at Salt Spring Seeds. There are quite a few details because there are many different kinds of seed. But when you consider that almost everything I know about seed saving is here, I hope you'll agree it's not that complicated and be enticed to save some of your own seeds.

Tools and Equipment

If you visited Mansell Farm, you'd probably be surprised at our unsophisticated seed-saving operation. We have a medium-size greenhouse where our seeds are taken after they are picked in the field. It's just an ordinary wood-frame greenhouse, measuring about 3.5 metres by 7 metres (12 feet by 22 feet) with lots of open wooden shelving. The greenhouse serves as our starting place for transplants in the spring. We try to get everything into the ground by mid-July, when the structure is converted officially to drying space. By August, various kinds of seeds to be stored are occupying various kinds of screens on the shelves, usually for only a day or two before they are threshed, cleaned, given additional drying time and then put away. Our drying screens are mostly of two sizes, 60 centimetres by 90 centimetres (two by three feet) and 30 centimetres by 30 centimetres (one foot by one foot), and are made of fabric screen sandwiched by a perimeter of screwed-together wood.

We also have an assortment of sifting screens of different gauges, obtained from hardware stores, garage sales and friends. In practice, we use only a few of these to separate seeds from chaff and debris.

Sitting in one corner of the drying greenhouse is our little air compressor. In terms of expense it is our one major tool, having cost us $300 new. It has a blow-nozzle attachment that squirts air under pressure. We use the air compressor to separate seeds from chaff for most of our crops. It does this remarkably quickly and efficiently because viable seeds are mostly heavier than the pods, hulls and other accoutrement that come with seed gathering.

We could survive without the air compressor, by using screens alone or by blowing away the chaff with a fan or hair dryer or even by winnowing the seeds in the wind.

Then there's our threshing box, described on page 56. We thresh with our feet all our beans and grains, plus all other seeds that are borne in pods, such as those of kale, flax and lupine. Once you perfect the technique, it takes less than a minute to crush and pop from their pods a box full of seeds and only a few minutes to rub the hulls off grains with your feet.

We have lots of plastic (11-litre) ice-cream pails, obtained from local stores for 50 cents each. We collect and store seeds in these, and we also use them to clean seeds with the air compressor after threshing.

We employ the ice-cream buckets to ferment tomatoes. This is the only part of our seed saving operation that requires water and we do have a water faucet in the greenhouse.

That's about it for seed-saving equipment, apart from indelible marking pens, labels and various containers to store the seeds.

Techniques

So come to Mansell Farm and see what we do during our long seed-saving season, bearing in mind that we're processing seed for 6,000 customers.

Legumes

First off, we have hundreds of seed varieties that come in pods. These include all the legumes we grow, such as regular beans, runner beans, peas, favas, chick-peas, soybeans, tepary beans, lentils and limas. Depending on variety, these dry down from July to October. Generally our focus is on those varieties that mature the earliest and we encourage our customers to grow those cultivars that will dependably dry down year after year in their gardens.

In the process of drying down, all these legumes lose their leaves until only the pods are left. Most get to the point where the beans rattle in the pods if you shake them. Some beans' pods twist open and spurt their seeds on hot days, so it's important to do daily checks when harvest is close. If your thumbnail can't make a dent in the seed, the beans are definitely ready.

We pick the pods by hand, gathering them in our buckets, and take them to our drying greenhouse where we spread them on the larger screens. Although they could be threshed immediately, we usually give them another drying day or two in case some seeds are not quite done.

After a hot day in the greenhouse, pods of most varieties will pop open with little pressure. Podding them in the threshing box is no arduous affair; it's mostly a stepping process, with the occasional shuffle to make sure you get all of them.

There are certainly alternatives to the threshing box. The seeds could be foot threshed in a tarp or in a burlap bag on any hard surface. Some sources recommend using a stick to thrash the beans. You could hand squish the pods quite quickly — gloves are recommended. (This process is actually closer to kneading; squeezing and cracking the dry pods with the fingers, the shelled beans quickly go to the bottom and the split pods stay on top.) Opening the pods one by one can be a very exciting as well as mesmerizing activity and is what I used to do before I made the threshing box.

Ambulating in the threshing box can also be quite thrilling. For us here at Mansell Farm, the satisfying crackling of the pods is followed by the squirts of compressed air that blow out all the open shells. In less than a minute, the sea of pods and pod pieces is out of the box and the beans are revealed in all their vibrant colours and designs.

Using the air nozzle to blow the debris from the seeds does take a bit of expertise. It's one of those skills you learn very quickly, however, because you don't want to spray the beans out of the box along with everything else. The air pressure goes down as you use it and builds up again if your finger is off the trigger. So you learn to adjust your distance.

There are other techniques that are almost inevitably developed if you go the air compressor route. Quick hand movements with the nozzle can really jiggle the chaff and get it up and away. Tilting the box allows the pods to be whisked away by the air currents.

Our plastic pails lend themselves even more effectively than our threshing box to seed cleaning with the air compressor. If you don't fill them more than one-third full (you want to have some of the bottom exposed when the pail is tilted toward you), you can create a great whirlwind effect that grabs everything except the seeds. Combining this with an intermittent up and down motion on the bucket cleans beans very quickly.

Lately, speedy person that I am, I've taken to doing most of the nozzle squirting in the threshing box, pouring the remains from the box into a pail and then finishing the process in the pail. This probably saves a minute or two (but we do have many hundreds of bean varieties).

When the beans are clean, they go back on their screen, either by upturning the box (it has handles at either end) or by pouring them out of the pail. Then they usually have another warm day of drying before being put away.

In most cases it's probably unnecessary to give the beans additional drying time after threshing and cleaning, but I've made it standard practice as a precautionary measure. It's easy to spot beans that aren't quite finished drying: they are slightly larger and their colours aren't as deep.

Once bean-drying time is in full swing, the greenhouse is usually a rich and changing feast for the eyes as the dance of musical beans goes on and on.

Having the shelled beans on the screens also facilitates selection and discarding (known as "roguing") of broken, munched or otherwise suspect beans. We usually get 100 percent germination with our beans because every tray is carefully inspected.

Even though we know our bean varieties very well, their identifying stick or marker always accompanies them. When they are put away in their buckets, glass jars or other containers, they get a sticky label noting the date.

Our seed storage place is an old country summer kitchen that stays cool and dry. The snug lids make the pails quite airtight, but beans actually like "breathing" once in a while, something our beans have ample opportunity to do with all the packaging that goes on.

We don't worry about our beans being subjected to cold winter weather. If they are adequately dry, frost does no damage. On the other hand, freezing temperatures kill any insects that have managed to hitchhike rides with the seeds.

Kept cool and dry, beans will easily stay viable for four or five years. Salt Spring Seeds always mails out the current year's stock of seed, but we often plant older seed here at the farm. For seed preservation purposes, you'd be safe growing out a variety one year out of four.

So that's pretty much our bean-saving story here at Salt Spring Seeds. Beans take up a lot of our time because we maintain so many different kinds and varieties, but they are certainly easy. How much more so for the home gardener, wanting to grow and maintain a few favourites, who can afford the leisure and pleasure of shucking them by hand.

Lettuce Seed

Let us check out our lettuce scenario now. Lettuces are easy, too. Like the beans, and as for many crops grown in temperate climates, maturity dates are quite significant. Many gardening catalogues proudly advertise that their lettuce cultivars are slow to bolt. That's okay if you want to depend on seed companies every year, but for the seed saver it's definitely not too fruitful.

If you want to be a saver of lettuce seed, it's best to find those cultivars that produce the kind of lettuce you want but also produce seed before the plants are frozen or rained out. In short-season growing areas, it might be necessary to start lettuces early indoors. With a good mulch, it's also possible to overwinter young lettuces in some places. Most of our lettuce seed is collected in September and October.

Lettuces are quite different from beans in the manner in which they complete their cycle. They don't dry down, they grow up. They put up a flowering stalk that can grow waist-high, and as they do so the leaves become shrunken versions of their former selves. The candelabra-like appearance of many cultivars is so attractive that we now take their aesthetic appeal into consideration when planning the garden.

A single lettuce can produce hundreds of small yellow flowers atop its stalk. The flowers become bunches of feathery little seed sites, each flower creating eight to 15 seeds. The seeds are a miniature version of dandelion seeds, having a tiny parachute perfect for riding the breezes. They are little wedges about one-third of a centimetre (an eighth of an inch long) and are either white or black, depending on variety.

Someone who wants to have enough seed for the next year could simply pluck two or three fuzzy seed heads to easily get a couple of dozen seeds, but we descend with our buckets. Even for us, eight or 10 plants is sufficient to provide all the seeds we need.

The seeds ripen over several weeks, and when they start there are still lots of blooming flowers. We usually wait until one-third of the seeds are ready, then collect them when conditions are dry.

As with most seed harvesting, people have different approaches. The plants can be rubbed between the hands or tipped into whatever container you're employing and shaken to release the seeds. I rub the seed heads between the thumb and fingers of my left hand while holding the bucket under them with my right. After doing this for a bit, I bend the part I have done into the pail and vigorously tap the branches back and forth against the sides. This releases seeds that have not yet fallen.

Pleasurable components of lettuce seed gathering deserve mention here — namely, the rhythmic tappity-tap-tap-tap of seed heads against the bucket and the satisfying thwack of the lettuces-to-be hitting the bottom.

After gathering, the seed is taken to the drying room, where it is poured and spread onto plates, pans or bucket lids. The freshly harvested seed usually comes with a little fluff and flower parts; the fluff dries quickly in the heat of the greenhouse.

After a few hours the seed is put back into the buckets, rubbed between the fingers to release the fluff and given a fast but careful spritzing with the air nozzle. Then it's poured onto and sifted through the appropriate screen and returned to its drying spot. Presto, the seeds are clean and will be ready to be put away the same day if there are a few more hours of heat left. Otherwise, we let them hang out in the greenhouse for a few hot hours the next day.

Again, identifying labels accompany the seeds at each step until the sticky labels are put on their containers. These are usually small jars or plastic boxes, since lettuce seeds take up so little space.

Our big plastic pails, strangely enough, are used to transport the seeds. Their malleability enables the pails to be bent at the top to create a convenient pouring spout. I cup my right hand around the jar and with my left pour the seeds through the funnel thus created. At the end I do a short drum flurry on the pails to make sure every last seedy character is out of the bucket.

That's the lettuce seed story here. And as simple as this is, the amateur seed saver could simply pluck some seed heads, make sure they're quite dry and store them in a dry container in a cool place.

Lettuce seeds stay viable for many years. I have successfully sown five-year-old seed.

Tomato Seed

Saving tomato seed can be totally simple, too; as elegantly easy as scooping a few seeds that slurped out of the homegrown tomatoes you were cutting and then putting them on a windowsill to dry.

There is an accepted tomato seed-saving method that is slightly more complicated. No one has yet convinced me of its total necessity, but I do it anyway because the few serious seed-saving books say you should. Letting ripe tomatoes ferment for a few days is supposed to prevent certain bacterial and viral diseases from persisting through the seed. (I wouldn't save seed from any tomato that was obviously diseased.)

Actually, fermenting tomatoes turns tomato seed saving into quite a juicy ritual.

We pick the tomatoes when they are really ripe in (you guessed it!) our large plastic ice-cream pails. Then we bring them to the drying greenhouse. We kneel on the grass outside the greenhouse and proceed to squish from the pulp as many seeds as possible, both seeds and pulp staying in the bucket. One soon finds out that cultivars vary considerably in their pulpiness.

Mushing and squeezing done, we get the garden hose and add a little more water so that all seeds and pulp are in the bath. As we're doing this we're watering seeds off our hands into the pail, so that nary a seed is around when we're scrunching the next variety.

Then we put the lid on, making sure our plastic marker with the tomato's name in indelible ink has not been left on the grass. The bucket goes on one of the lower shelves in the greenhouse and we repeat the process for all the tomato varieties we've just collected.

Three days later we go and observe the mouldy, fermented brew. (You're not supposed to let the fermenting process go on much longer.) We take the bucket outside and begin hosing back into the liquid whatever seeds are still attached to the tomato meat. As we do this we discard the pulp over the side to be later composted. After the tomato pieces have been rinsed, we pause for a few seconds as the last of the seeds sink to the bottom.

Then we gently pour the liquid out of the bucket and watch all the remaining bits of skin and flesh float over the edge. Ta-dah! There are all the tomato seeds on the bottom!

It can take a couple of tippings to get the liquid to come completely clear.

The next thing is to pour the clear water and the seeds onto one of our small screens. It's a skill to do this in one go. Usually a few seeds will be left in the pail and it will be necessary to add some more water and do another pour.

The seeds tend to clump up on the screen. Spraying with the hose gets them evenly spread for faster drying.

The seeds dry remarkably fast. On a sunny day, if you put them on the screens in the morning you can be storing them away in the late afternoon.

In the middle of the day, when the seeds are already mostly dry, I scrape them gently off the screen with their plastic marker to aerate them a bit more. I also rub them between my fingers to separate seeds that are stuck together.

The seeds turn a very light colour when dry. They look and feel dry. Some sources of seed-saving information say to let them dry for two weeks (as they do for lettuce seed), but I feel that one sunny day in the greenhouse is sufficient. I've seen lots of tomato mould but have yet to see any mouldy tomato seeds.

Our dry tomato seeds get poured one last time into the buckets (which have been drying themselves, upside down on the highest greenhouse shelves) and then funnelled, like our lettuce seed, into small containers. They, too, easily remain viable for five years.

Cucumbers are our only other crop that goes through anything like a fermentation process. Other seeds that are contained by the "fruit" of the plant, such as peppers, eggplant, melons and squash are simply scooped onto drying screens.

For most of the rest of our seeds the method of saving is similar to how we obtain bean and lettuce seed. Our grains are threshed by feet in our wooden box and it takes a few minutes longer to rub off hulls than it does to pop pods. The threshing box works very quickly and efficiently for the likes of flax, kale and lupine seed. Our flower and herb seeds are plucked, shaken or tipped into the buckets when the seed heads have totally dried and then they get a further drying, followed by spritzing and/or sifting and yet a further drying.

When you collect flower and herb seeds you quickly discover that, despite the plants being spent, seed heads are action central for an amazing host of insects. I recommend an outdoor space for first putting seeds on drying screens or trays, instead of having all the bugs skedaddling in your house!

Amaranth

The only seed we collect while plants are still flowering is amaranth. I have found over the years that it is more practical and efficient to get amaranth seeds before the plants die down. I've described the seed-saving process for amaranth on pages 139–40.

Harvesting fresh seed from still-flowering plants means seeds have more drying to do. It's most important to further dry your crop to ensure it won't mould in storage. I usually leave amaranth seeds on trays for three hot days, stirring occasionally until they are as dry as possible. Store seed in airtight containers in a cool, dry place.

Quinoa

Quinoa, so similar to amaranth in many ways, is harvested like most of our other crops. It is ready to pick when the leaves have fallen, leaving just the dried seed heads. Seeds can be easily stripped upward off the stalk with a gloved hand.

Quinoa is adapted to conditions of such low moisture that, if rained on, the mature seed can germinate. So sometimes we harvest quinoa just a little early, if it is almost ready and extended rainfall is forecast.

We don't bring other crops indoors to complete their drying except at the very end of the season, or if birds are significantly munching away. We do this by pulling entire plants and hanging them upside down in our greenhouse. As long as the crop is close to maturity, the seeds will continue to ripen.

General Harvest Notes

Seeds of most plants dry right down in field or garden. However, it is a good rule of thumb to let harvested seed dry for at least a few more days after being removed from the plant. The larger the seed, the longer the drying period required. Most seeds will dry adequately for home storage if spread on paper towels, newspapers or screens in an airy place for a few days to a week. They should be turned and spread several times and the paper changed if wet.

An equally good drying method is to let the seed heads or stalks dry in open paper bags for one or two weeks. The drying process can be hastened by spreading the seed in a sun-exposed room, in a nonhumid greenhouse or in the sun outside if the seed is covered or brought in at night. Lacking sun and/or greenhouse, you can speed drying with gentle heat so long as the temperature never rises above 38°C (100°F).

General Storage Notes

Seed should always be stored under cool, dry conditions. Temperatures well below freezing will not harm seeds if they have been adequately dried. Viability is increased by sealing most seeds from air, except in the case of beans and peas, which like some "open air."

Most sound vegetable seeds, if stored properly, will remain viable for many years, with the exception of short-lived onion, leek, corn and parsnip seed.

Put each kind of seed into its own envelope, with the cultivar name and the date of storage noted. You can also put envelopes or simply the seeds in airtight tins, glass jars or plastic containers that can be closed to make them moisture-proof.

Longevity can be increased by storing seed containers in a freezer.

Apart from the actual picking, processing and preserving of seeds, it is most helpful to know if a crop is an annual, biennial or perennial, and whether it is self-pollinated or cross-pollinated.

Plant Types and Specifics

Let's go through all of the seed crops at Salt Spring Seeds, but this time classify them as to when they go to seed and whether you have to worry about the seed staying true. First, a few definitions:

- **Annual** plants flower and mature seed in the same year.
- **Biennial** plants are normally harvested as food in their first summer or fall but do not flower or produce seed until the next year. In mild coastal or southern areas, biennials will survive the winter under a cover of mulch. In most of continental North America biennials must be dug up and carefully stored during the winter, to be replanted in the spring. Most biennials become tall and bushy when going to seed, taking up more space than they did the previous year. They can be thinned or transplanted to twice the usual spacing.
- **Perennials** live and bear seed year after year.

Self-versus Cross-Pollination

Pollination is the process by which pollen grains are carried from one plant part to another.

- In **self-pollinated** plants this process occurs within each flower, with no pollen being transferred from one flower to another on the same plant or between plants. Such flowers have both male and female parts and pollination occurs successfully within the single bloom. The seeds of these plants almost always retain the quality of the parent seed, or stay "true." Because they rarely cross with another variety of the same species, isolating them is unnecessary unless absolute purity in a strain is desired.

- Most other familiar vegetables are **cross-pollinated** — the pollen from one flower fertilizes another flower, either on the same or another plant. The pollen is carried by wind or insects. It is important to know the other varieties of the same species with which a plant has the potential to exchange pollen. Allowing only one variety of each potentially cross-pollinating vegetable to flower out eliminates the need to separate plants from each other. As well, barriers can be erected or planted, plantings can be staggered or crops can be covered with garden fabric.

Self-pollinating Annuals

Many self-pollinating annuals already been discussed in detail: **beans, grains, lettuces and tomatoes** form the bulk of the fun for us Salt Spring Seeders. It is so easy to save such a diversity of them.

There are three kinds of beans that, because of their more open flowers, can be pollinated by insects as well as by themselves: **runner beans, fava beans** and **lima beans**. If you have an active bee population, you might see a new bean colour when you grow out your saved seeds. To maintain purity in these bean families, it is best to grow only one variety of each or to separate them as much as possible.

You can occasionally get surprise seeds with other beans and it's hard to know whether a cross has occurred or a genetic throwback. I call these "throwforwards" because they can be most interesting to grow out. You can lessen the already remote chances of such offerings by alternating bean rows by families or maturity dates.

Favas ripen over a longer period than most beans. The pods at the base of the stalk blacken first. The home gardener can wait to pick until half the pods have dried black, usually by the end of July. It takes several weeks for all the pods to dry, necessitating two or three pickings.

We've yet to get a lettuce or tomato cross at Mansell Farm, but it's advisable to not allow undomesticated lettuce varieties such as wild or prickly lettuce to flower nearby.

For some heading varieties of lettuce, such as iceberg and Great Lakes, it helps to peel back the matured heads' leaves to expose the growing point and liberate the flowering stalk.

Eggplants should be allowed to mature on the plant past the edible stage. Cut the fruit in half, scoop out the seeds and wash them free from pulp by stirring them in water. They will separate and sink to the bottom. Don't ferment them, but dry them immediately in thin layers on paper or screen. If after drying they are stuck together, rub them gently to separate them. Seeds remain viable for only a year or two.

Peppers are treated as self-pollinating annuals although they are perennials in warm climates. Most bell peppers ripen a rich red. A few fruit will supply seed for hundreds of plants. Remove the seed mass, allow it to air dry and rub it to separate the seed. Alternatively, wash the seed with water in an appropriate container; the debris will float and the seeds can be immediately dried by spreading them out in the sun or in a warm place indoors.

Because self-pollinated plants inbreed automatically, you can generally use as many plants of the above crops as you wish for seed purposes. Seed from exceptional single plants, however, could be saved separately to increase the chance of retaining its special characteristics.

Cross-pollinated Annuals

For cross-pollinated plants, it is important to maintain vigour by saving seed from at least several individual plants of the same variety, even if you need only a few seeds. In any planting, cross-pollinated vegetables may look identical but some will be genetically different. Saving seed from only one or two plants, known as inbreeding, severely reduces necessary genetic contributions and results in reduced vigour and yield in succeeding generations. (Exceptions to this rule are squashes and pumpkins, which do not noticeably lose vigour even if inbred for several generations.) Roguing must be done before plants flower.

Broccoli is most often treated as an annual, but overwintering varieties can be allowed to flower and set seed the following spring and summer. For annual broccoli, an early-spring sowing is recommended. Broccoli is normally cross-pollinated by bees, so it is best to grow only one variety or isolate two or more varieties. Broccoli as a member of the Brassica family will cross with cabbage, brussels sprouts, cauliflower, collards, kale and kohlrabi, so must not be flowering at the same time as any of these (which is unlikely to happen unless you are also saving seed of one or more of them).

As for other brassicas, broccoli seed is borne in narrow pods. Harvest when pods are dry and brittle. Plant stalks can be laid on tarps or canvas for further curing outside, or branches of pods can be placed in open paper bags and dried in the sun.

Threshing can be done by hand, flailing, or by rubbing the seedpods gently through screen. We normally snip the seed stalks and immediately thresh them by foot in our box.

Corn is cross-pollinated by the wind so isolation is essential. Any one corn (sweet, ornamental, dent, flint, flour or popcorn) will cross very easily with any other and a neighbour's corn should be at least a half kilometre (one-quarter mile) away. Late and early varieties can be planted beside each other if the first variety sheds its pollen before the silks appear on the second. Harvest when cobs are dry and give them additional drying under cover. Husks of six to eight ears can be tied together and hung in an airy place. When seeds are sufficiently dry, it is usually easy to hold an ear in one hand and twist off the kernels with the other. The kernels can also be left on the cobs to be displayed through the winter. Storage life is only a year or two.

Because corn is such an inbreeder, most sources recommend growing a minimum of 100 plants to ensure genetic diversity.

Cucumbers are pollinated mainly by bees, do cross with one another, but don't cross with other vine crops. Let the fruits ripen past the edible stage, when they will become golden, yellow or white. It doesn't matter if the vines are killed by frost. Slice the fruits in half lengthwise and scoop the pulp and seeds into a nonmetallic container. Leave the mixture in a warm place and stir it a few times daily. Fermentation will reduce the jelly-like pulp around each seed to a thin liquid and will be complete in three or four days. The best seeds will sink to the bottom of the container and the lighter, inferior ones will rise to the top. Pour off the floating seeds, wash those remaining by stirring them in a few changes of water or washing them in a sieve, then spread them on paper or screens. Dry them outdoors in sunny weather or in a warm airy room, stirring periodically to encourage uniform drying, until they feel rough but not slippery to the touch.

Squash and **pumpkins** are also pollinated by bees. The four different species won't cross species or cross with cucumbers and melons. *Cucurbita pepo* includes all common summer squashes, all acorn types, the orange pumpkin types, Delicata, Lady Godiva and spaghetti. *C. maxima* includes buttercup, Hubbard, Delicious, banana and Hokkaido. *C. moschata* includes butternut and cheese types. *Cucurbita mixta* includes the cushaw squashes. All will cross with their own species members.

Fastening paper bags over the female flowers, then dabbing pollen from male flowers onto the female and closing the bag again until the chance of cross-pollination is over, ensures genetic integrity. At Mansell Farm, we don't do the pollinating and tend to grow one representative of each species each growing season.

Summer squash must be left on the vine for about eight weeks past its normal harvesting date until the skin becomes as hard as that of winter squash. All squash and pumpkin seed will gain vigour if allowed to afterripen in the fruit. Removing and storing them can wait for a month or two. They may be left past the first fall frost.

Cut the fruit of the mature pumpkin or squash in half. Remove the seeds and moist material around them with a large spoon, place it all in a large bowl, add some water and work the mixture through the fingers. The seeds will separate gradually. Wash them again and spread them out on paper or screens to dry for a week or more, moving them about daily so they don't remain in small, wet piles. Cull out any flat seeds: only the plump ones are viable.

If kept in a sealed jar, check them after a few weeks to see if there is any sign of moisture. If so, take them out for additional drying.

Spinach has a very fine pollen that can be carried 1.5 kilometres (three-quarters of a mile) or more by the wind. Rogue or remove plants that bolt to seed without producing good spinach. Spinach seed normally ripens unevenly in the latter part of summer. Strip mature seeds from the stalks with your hands.

Amaranth and **quinoa** are also cross-pollinated annuals. They will cross with their wild relatives, so it is important to weed out red-rooted pigweed and lamb's-quarter if you want to maintain pure seed. Amaranth cultivars will cross with each other, as will quinoa cultivars, so grow only one kind of each or separate the cultivars by as much distance as you can. Certain varieties, such as purple-leaved amaranth, are easier to select for than others. Lamb's-quarter has a greater branching habit than quinoa and smaller flower heads.

Cross-pollinated Biennials

These vegetables produce their edible crop in the first season and their flowers and seeds in the second. As they need overwintering to complete their cycle, they can be left in the ground or brought indoors, depending on location and preference.

Plant seed of the following **biennial root crops** early enough that the plants will be mature at the end of the growing season. When digging up plants for storage, choose healthy specimens that show characteristics desirable in the variety. Don't save seed from plants that bolt to seed in the first season.

It is beneficial to prepare roots for storage by curing. This is a process that dries and toughens the skin but leaves the root firm and plump. Curing enables the root to resist moulding and heals small breaks in the skin that would otherwise invite decay. Harvest the roots on a dry day, when the soil isn't too wet. Gently shake or rub off any excess earth. Cut the tops off about 2.5 centimetres (one inch) above the crown and then lay them to dry, either in the sun for a few hours or indoors for a day or so. Turn them once, so that all parts are exposed to air.

Beets are cross-pollinated by the wind. The pollen is very light and can be carried long distances, so it is best to raise seed of only one variety each year. If you bring your beets indoors, pull them in the fall before heavy frosts. Cut their tops 2.5 centimetres (one inch) above the crown. Handle beets carefully, as damaged ones may rot. Three beets are adequate for most needs.

Your storage system should provide even moisture to prevent the beets from shrivelling. A storage temperature of 4 to 10°C (40 to 50°F) favours subsequent seed stalk production more than a temperature closer to freezing. A good storage method is to layer beets in a box between dampened sand or fresh sawdust.

We always leave our beets in the ground over winter and protect them from frost with a thick layer of mulch.

In the second year, beets should be thinned or replanted to about 60 centimetres (two feet) apart, the crowns even with the soil surface. As with just about any seed crop, you'll be amazed by how many seeds are produced by one plant. Beet seeds are actually seed balls, each containing up to six seeds. In summer, when plants are completely dry with brown, mature seeds, seed balls are easily stripped by hand from the branches.

Swiss chard produces seed stalks similar to beets. Beets and Swiss chard will cross with each other, so avoid saving seeds from both crops in the same season (which of course doesn't prevent you from growing both for food). Swiss chard is extremely hardy and, for seed-saving purposes, there is usually no need to dig up and store the plants.

Carrots are cross-pollinated by a variety of insects. They will cross readily with Queen Anne's lace, so it's important to keep this wild plant clipped so it doesn't flower when carrots do. Carrots and parsnips do not cross.

Carrots can be harvested in the fall before the ground freezes, leafy tops cut to 2.5 centimetres (one inch), and stored at high humidity and near-freezing temperatures. Some people cut off only the crown or top 2.5 centimetres (one inch) of the plant for replanting. They can be kept in boxes of damp sand or sawdust. In the spring, replant carrots 30 centimetres (one foot) apart.

In mild areas carrots can be left in the ground under thick mulch. In cold areas they will often survive outside under heavy snow cover.

Carrots grow up to two metres (six feet) high in the second year. Each has a large head with a series of branches beneath it. The flower heads are given the name "umbel" to describe flower clusters in which stalks, nearly equal in length, spring from a common centre. Seed umbels mature unevenly; it's best to harvest when secondary heads have ripe brown seed and third-order heads are starting to turn brown. This is usually around September of the second year. Heads can be removed as they mature, or entire stalks can be cut and cured for a few weeks. Rub off seeds when completely dry and use a screen to remove the chaff.

Leeks are pollinated by honeybees. They may cross with onions. Generally they overwinter easily. Early tall-stemmed summer types should be hilled up with soil or mulched heavily. Rogue and eat the less desirable plants in the fall. In the second year, individual plants will send up single stalks 1.2 to 1.5 metres (four to five feet) high capped by beautiful, huge umbels composed of hundreds of flowers. In the fall, when you see the seeds inside their capsules, pick the heads and further dry them well. Brisk rubbing will extract the seeds.

Onions are also pollinated by honeybees and do cross with each other. Harvest them as usual in fall; rogue double onions and those with thick necks. As onions are not heavy seed producers, choose 12 to 15 of your best bulbs. Larger bulbs will produce more seed. Prepare your onions for storage by curing them as you do your eating onions. Check that the neck area, where the tops join the bulb, is shrivelled and well dried. The best storage conditions are dry, airy and cool. Be careful not to bruise or injure the bulbs, and replant them as early in spring as possible. In mild areas, and especially with sweet onions that don't store well, it is better to leave the plants in the soil over winter. Cover the bulb, leaving its top barely exposed.

Large flower heads above stalks around one metre (3 feet) tall develop over several weeks in summer. Start harvesting when the fruits open to expose the black seed. Cut off the umbels as they become ready and dry them in trays or bags, on screen or canvas, in sun or under cover, stirring them occasionally. Seed should dry to the point that is easily rubbed from the heads. Drying will often take over two weeks. Seed life is only a year or two.

Parsnips are hardy cross-pollinated biennials that are usually planted in the spring in cold climates and in midsummer in mild areas. As with carrots, you can choose to replant only the crowns. The mature seed is dry and light brown by the next summer and shatters, or falls off the plant readily, so harvest should not be delayed.

The other main cross-pollinating biennials are **brassicas. Brussels sprouts, cabbage, collards, cauliflower, kale** and **kohlrabi** are members of the cabbage family that, like broccoli, are pollinated mainly by bees and cross-pollinate readily. They require isolation from other family members and from other varieties of themselves for true seed. Unlike (most) broccoli, they must be overwintered outside or taken into storage conditions of high humidity and near-freezing temperatures. When replanted in spring, plants should be set 60 to 90 centimetres (two to three feet) apart. For cabbages, it is common practice to make crosscuts about 2.5 centimetres (one inch) deep into the top centre of each head to facilitate emergence of the seed stalk. Staking keeps cabbages, which grow to 1.5 metres (five feet) the second year, from falling over. Cauliflower is the most difficult of the cabbage family to raise from seed in cold climates, because most varieties do not overwinter well either indoors or under thick mulch outdoors.

Pods of all the brassicas burst open as they become dry and brittle, so harvesting them a little early and curing them further in paper bags or on trays is a good way to avoid losing any seed. Storage life of brassica seed is about five years.

Perennials

Chives are pollinated by bees. They don't cross with onions or leeks. Cut off the seed heads when the seeds blacken. Allow to further dry for a few weeks, then rub off the seeds with your hands.

Asparagus is usually grown from the roots or crowns but can also be grown from seed. The seed is ready to harvest in the fall, when the asparagus berries turn red and the ferny top leaves flop over.

Cut off asparagus tops and hang to dry. Soak the berries in water for an hour, until you can easily remove the pulp from the seed. Spread the seed on a tray and keep in a warm, dry, airy place until thoroughly dry.

Rhubarb is usually grown from root sections of established plants. Not many varieties produce seed heads. The large seed disks of those that do can be gathered and dried in the usual ways.

Clonal Reproduction

Potatoes, sunroot (also known as Jerusalem artichokes) and **garlic** are saved through their tubers or bulbs. The genetic makeup of a cultivated variety of any of these stays the same, although they can demonstrate quite different adaptations to soil and locale. Most people know there are lots of different kinds of potatoes, but few realize there are dozens of distinct sunroot and garlic cultivars that vary in taste, appearance, productivity, et cetera.

Potato plants sometimes produce seeds, but normally they are of no use to the seed saver since they will not produce true. Choose only healthy plants for reproduction, because it is particularly easy for diseases to be passed from one generation to the next. A few hours of drying outside toughens the skins for storage. How well potatoes keep doesn't seem to be affected by washing or not washing them. Burying them in dry sand is an excellent storage method. They should be kept in the dark.

Sunroot tubers start forming with the onset of cold weather in September or October and keep growing after the visible plant has blackened and died. Sunroots are most delicious after the first frosts hit them and remain so until sprouting begins in spring. They are tricky to store because their thin skin causes them to shrivel easily. It's best to simply leave them in the ground until you want to use them, either for food or "seed."

It is advisable to start digging inward at more than 30 centimetres (one foot) from the stalk to avoid mutilating the tubers, which grow on lateral shoots. However, sunroots are notorious for being able to sprout new growth from even the tiniest pieces of themselves.

We are often asked if our "seed" garlic can be eaten as well as planted. Of course, food stock and seed stock are more or less the same thing, although we do save our biggest bulbs for planting, both for our customers and for ourselves.

Except for eating purposes, garlic is out of the ground for only three or four months a year: it is usually harvested in late July and replanted in October. Not much can go wrong in those few months if you dry the bulbs well. Garlic keeps better in bulbs rather than separated into cloves, so it's best to take the bulbs apart shortly before planting.

Flowers and Herbs

Flowers and herbs go to seed in numerous ways and it's sometimes fascinating to figure out where exactly the seeds are, as well as the most efficient way of harvesting them. Usually seeds are easily shaken or stripped by hand into a bucket. At times you have to get there before the birds or the wind.

Most garden flowers are cross-pollinated by insects, so if you wish to preserve the purity of a certain strain for seed saving grow only one variety at a time, stagger plantings considerably or set up appropriate insect barriers.

Echinacea is one of our most important seed crops. It is also one of the trickiest because it's late to flower and the chaff is hard to clean. Seed of echinacea isn't ready until the flowers dry down in September or October. They slip from the central cone with a little nudge from the thumb. It is much better to harvest them during a dry spell. It is also wise to give them some additional drying in a sunny protected spot before storing them in glass jars or plastic containers. Brown chaff from the flowerheads is difficult to screen from the seeds because of similar size but it is not crucial for the amateur seed saver to remove it.

Echinacea seeds will germinate better if subjected to freezing temperatures for a few weeks.

Selection Criteria

I've tried to present seed-saving methods as uncomplicated as they have been for myself for the past 14 years. People without sophisticated training have been successfully saving seeds for the past 10,000 years. It's ironic that it's people with so-called scientific backgrounds who are creating the possible annihilation of seeds as we've known them.

For corporate researchers these days, the most sought-after trait in plants is their ability to withstand applications of poisons produced by the researchers' corporate bosses.

Many gardeners simply want to preserve their longtime favourite vegetables. Some growers also want to improve their crops. Nearly everyone has a different concept of what is ideal. Depending on needs and preferences, criteria for selection may include any of the following: flavour, size, resistance to disease, drought and/or insects, lateness or earliness to bolt, trueness to type, colour, shape, thickness of flesh, hardiness or storability. Selecting for such qualities is simply a matter of selecting for such qualities!

For most combinations of characteristics you're looking for, remember to consider the whole plant. Here at Mansell Farm we often select for yield by saving seed of the three or four highest-producing plants. The yield of most open-pollinated crops is considerably less than it used to be because companies simply don't spend time with less lucrative nonhybrids.

We also select for taste, especially with beans and garlic. We cook three or four pots of bean varieties and compare their flavours without salt or other seasoning. For garlic we usually organize raw taste tests with groups that visit the farm; we are always surprised by the degree of consensus.

To read the few significant seed-saving books available on the market might leave you with the feeling that it is crucial to maintain genetic purity. Such responsibility need be taken on only if you are officially preserving a named variety. If you grow two bean, lettuce or tomato varieties side by side, for example, and crossing does occur, it is almost certain that your new bean, lettuce or tomato will taste just as good as either parent. And it might have some useful characteristics neither parent had. (On the other hand, crosses between squash varieties, for example, invariably do produce inferior fruit.)

When I first started growing beans, I never saw crosses or throwforwards. Now I usually see three to six a year and frequently receive samples from other gardeners. To me this reflects accelerated planetary changes and seems to say that nature is more open than ever. Traditionally, agricultural societies have maintained a broad genetic base ("land races") for each of their crops, ensuring survival of some plants in the event of disease, pests or freak weather conditions. With extreme and unpredictable changes in the natural and social worlds, identical plants are now more vulnerable than ever. Most vulnerable of all are the monoculture crops on the vast acreages planted by corporate agriculture.

Smaller-scale farmers and gardeners are always in touch with their plants and have much greater flexibility to embrace changes as they occur. If nature is now throwing out more crosses and genetic sports than ever, we should receive the message and seize the exciting opportunity to grow out such plants.

Two bean selections in Salt Spring Seeds' catalogue, Child's Delight and Mansell Magic, are the result of new bean colours and colour combinations that appeared in our garden. To me, moving with nature's artistry is diametrically opposed to combining genes to create mutants that would never occur naturally. Not only are we already blessed with all the plants we need to feed the planet, there are many more that are continually being offered for our nourishment and delight.

Aesthetic Dimensions of Seed Saving

Seed saving not only lightens our living on the land by grounding us in the reality of what completes the circle of growing, it also enhances and beautifies the garden in configurations of maturing plants that have yet to be explored in gardening books and catalogues.

The more seeds I learn to save, the more delighted I am by aesthetic rewards inherent in growing garden crops to the seed stage.

Some common vegetables, such as onions, leeks, lettuces, endives, kales and chicories, become very different when they flower and then go to seed. Leaves change shape, stalks shoot skyward, flowers contrast with foliage, seed heads pop into existence; plants become hardly recognizable as the vegetables you were eating. As you get to know the colours, shapes and sizes to expect, you can incorporate your seed plants into overall garden design and even choose varieties for specific effects.

Our Russian kale seed plants have added a beautifully enriching mauve tinge to the pinks and purples of our back flower garden; the huge globular seed heads of our elephant leeks have been regal against maturing kamut; the candelabra-like effect of our flowering cressonnette Marocaine lettuces has been mesmerizing in our circle garden. Now we consciously try to plan such combinations in the same way we do more usual garden ornamentals.

There are also the unplanned combinations that appear from plants saved for seed. Seeds often escape the seed saver's attempts to collect them all, and volunteer plants of favourite vegetables and flowers may pop up in new places. Sometimes these volunteers appear even earlier than greenhouse sowings and usually they are more vigorous and better adapted than pampered transplants. Often they locate themselves in spots that delight the eye and warm the heart. Ever-more-beautiful gardens can come from learning to anticipate and play with such gratuitous offerings.

CHAPTER TWELVE

Strategies for Safeguarding Our Food and Our Seeds

The three divisions of this book — organic food, whole food, safe food — are each their own worlds. Yet they go together because organic food is increasingly the only safe food choice and organic whole foods are what sustain us best.

So the obvious first step in maintaining our mutual food security is to go organic, buy organic, support organic. And the obvious second step is to get to know beans and grains as well as other whole foods. What I believe to be the third step is not as obvious: it's about calling a spade a spade in terms of what's happening on this planet and putting our own spade deep in the ground.

There is so much promotion of "globalization" and "free trade" these days that there seems to be an inevitability and a rightness to the politics and processes these words represent. But hold on a second, let's look at what's really happening. Transnational corporations have become so powerful that they've been calling all the economic shots. As with their earlier "green revolution" agriculture that gave us deserts where once there was farmland, their "free trade" gives them the freedom to trade wherever and whenever they can make the most bucks. Everyone else is free only to be exploited.

What the transnationals call globalization is not about safeguarding our food; it will definitely not ensure a planet where our children will enjoy as rich and as wholesome a life as we would like. To grow poisoned, mutated food where labour is cheapest and rights are nonexistent and to then transport it thousands of kilometres is bad news for everyone's health and well being.

It is time to become aware of the impact of our food systems and choices, so as to live more lightly on the land. Even once to see what it takes to put food on our plates is often all it takes to change old eating habits. Pursuing the path of unconscious consumption has translated into heavy social and ecological problems. Yet if, in our daily actions, each of us takes our neighbours and our environment fully into account, sustainability can become a reality. Our food choices are very crucial.

When we buy products grown thousands of kilometres away and/or with the use of petrochemical fertilizers, biocides and bioengineering, we support the following:
• agribusiness and monoculture
• depletion of soil fertility
• soil erosion
• displacement of small-scale and family farms
• use of nonrenewable natural resources
• destruction of wildlife habitats and essential tropical rainforests
• increasing chronic and severe health problems of people working with these

chemicals and eating foods grown and treated with them

- increasing health and environmental problems resulting from agricultural chemical runoff into groundwater

When we buy local, organically grown food or eat our own, we are endorsing:

- high-quality nutrition
- food diversity and thus food security
- soil-saving and enrichment techniques
- stronger, more stable local economies
- energy efficiency and fewer trucks on the highways
- preservation of a sustainable environment for all Earth's inhabitants

Meat and Dairy

Meat and dairy products can be and are being produced using the same principles and practices as those used to raise organic vegetables.

Unfortunately, these same products are still overwhelmingly industrially farmed in ever-worsening conditions. The huge factory farms that raise animals for milk, cheese, butter, eggs and meat are exceedingly overcrowded and unsanitary. Animals are stuffed in stalls and cages by the tens and hundreds of thousands and driven literally crazy by deprivation, disease and mutilation. To prevent loss of stock and ultimate profit, these farms are routinely doused with highly toxic chemicals to kill the parasites that breed in such conditions. Bacterial infections such as salmonellosis are rampant, and endless rounds of antibiotics create new strains of invincible bacteria.

Most of the toxic biocides in our diet come from meat and dairy products. These foods end up on our plates replete also with growth and appetite stimulants, tranquilizers and steroid hormones. These are shocking facts; a powerful meat and dairy lobby plus our own disconnection from what we eat has kept them from being widely acknowledged until recently. Packaged meat and dairy foods may appear sanitary but, in reality, eating them exposes our bodies to unprecedented combinations of chemicals and poisons.

Plant versus Animal Protein

If we raised meat and dairy animals in safe and sane ways, and if we ate more beans and grains, our bodies would be much healthier. Cholesterol and saturated fat, found primarily in meat and dairy products, raise the level of cholesterol in the blood, cause obesity, produce hardening of the arteries and lead directly to heart disease and strokes. No risk factor for cancer is more significant than diet. Excessive protein consumption increases the risk of diabetes, arthritis, kidney deterioration, multiple sclerosis, ulcers, chronic constipation, osteoporosis and hypoglycemia.

Statistics also readily show that our Earth would be a lot less stressed if we reduced the scale of meat and dairy production. It is estimated that 85 percent of topsoil loss in North America is directly associated with raising livestock. Seven out of eight hectares of forest that are destroyed on this continent are used to graze livestock and/or grow livestock feed. Half of all the water consumed in North America goes to irrigate land that supports feed and fodder for livestock. And that doesn't include the enormous amounts used to wash animal excrement away — water that returns to and contaminates our water supply.

A half hectare (one and one-quarter) of land can produce about 75 kilograms (165 pounds) of beef, whereas the same area could produce 900 kilograms (2,000 pounds) of soybeans. The production of a half kilogram (one pound) of beef requires 11,000 (2,500 gallons) of water, compared with 110 litres (25 gallons) for the same amount of quinoa.

There are other questions concerning our meat and dairy industries in North America that are equally crucial to consider: What are the consequences to our health when we eat food from animals kept and slaughtered in states of fear, anger and panic? How can such a disharmonious, uncompassionate relationship with beings who share our planet possibly nurture us?

Perhaps the most poignant question of all is whether we are seriously addressing world food hunger when the livestock population of North America consumes enough grain and beans annually to feed the global population many times over.

Local and Organic

Examining the hidden costs of all our food choices is essential if we are to move toward a sustainable world. Lethal pesticides and herbicides that are banned in North America are still produced and sold to other countries and come right back to us in our imported avocados, bananas, tomatoes, melons, coffee and chocolate. The process by which once self-supporting nations have become impoverished and denuded in order to feed our coffee, banana, meat and sugar addictions threatens the well-being of every global citizen.

Much of this book is about healthful, nourishing foods that we can grow in our backyards in ways that are ecologically sound. Gardening is by far the most popular leisure-time activity in North America. Already some 75 million of us spend lots of time and money caring for the bit of nature surrounding our homes. By committing ourselves to our own health and that of our communities we can go a long way toward helping to restore economic and ecological balance on a planetary scale.

By becoming more conscious of what we grow and consume, we take greater responsibility for ourselves and our families. We can learn to discriminate between our real needs and our desires. We can respect the rights of others to exist healthfully within their own habitats. We can attune to ways of producing and sharing food locally, and we can foster trade based on reciprocity, mutual benefit and cooperation. Tuning in to the inherent sustainability of our immediate ecosystem fosters the ultimate sustainability of our planet. Indeed, the best place to begin is at home.

Sustainability, when it comes right down to it, speaks to an ability and a dedication to keep growing on our same patch of earth.

SEEDING COMMUNITY

Choices for a sustainable lifestyle are open to each individual, but the concept of sustainability embraces more than individualized response. Taking care of ourselves needs to be wedded to being cared for. If we are to keep our planet green, we must join the circle to maintain its integrity, we must reach out to participate in its wholeness. Hands to hold are everywhere around us and, as the saying goes, "Many hands make light work."

Whether our focus is personal or transpersonal, social or political, regional, national or cultural, we can make a difference by acting on the realization that we are all in this together.

Community Gardens

Land still available in urban and suburban areas can be utilized for food growing to a much greater extent than at present.

In the Second World War, many people who were left at home facing reduced availability of food proudly joined together to create what were called "Victory" gardens. Today most North American cities, following the European model, have what are called "allotment" gardens. These municipally organized plots of land enable people who otherwise would not have access to a patch of earth to grow fruit and vegetables in the midst of a city or town. Such community gardens are testaments to what is possible when there is a strong need or desire to grow food.

An abundance of food can be grown in small spaces. Even an outside patio or apartment balcony can be the site of substantial growing endeavours. The foods described in this book, however, are most efficiently grown with friends and neighbours in gardens that are at least large enough to plant a packet of beans or grain. This is how I've been fortunate to grow my gardens for the last few years. This is the direction my own food growing has been taking and I know of many other families who are combining energies in similar ways. It is so easy and enjoyable to hoe, weed and harvest the likes of beans, quinoa and amaranth with other enthusiasts. It is also very special to share the exquisite and substantial nourishment of meals made with these foods.

These high-protein crops can be grown in urban settings by expanding the concept of allotment gardens with their small family plots to include common areas managed by more people. Such a pooling of space would also make it more practical to maintain soil fertility and tilth with green manures and cover crops.

Cooperative approaches can also work well in suburban areas. Families with extra space can share some with neighbours who have none. Adjacent families, both with backyard gardens, can alternate food and cover crops yearly. One rototiller and one chipper/shredder can serve all the people on a suburban block. Community compost piles can provide usable compost more quickly than individual ones because of their greater volume.

Whenever people join together for a common purpose it means that the weight of the project rests on no one person's shoulders. Whether in city or country, community gardens invite people to pitch in with their best skills and to nurture each other as well as the garden.

Community Shared Agriculture

Community shared agriculture is such a great idea that it's amazing it took until the

1990s to take hold. The notion is simple: basically, consumers enter into an agreement with a farmer to obtain produce on a regular basis. Farmers get the security of assured sales and customers get the security of knowing where their food comes from.

Many arrangements are possible. Usually shares are sold and money is paid-upfront for an entire season. Deliveries are often weekly and can be at drop-off points or at individual residences; or pick-up can be at the farm. Sometimes part of the agreement is to work some hours at the farm.

Community shared agriculture joins farm folk and city folk in healthy and happy mutual growth. People appreciate clean, wholesome food as well as a direct connection to the country, and farmers appreciate their appreciation. It's no wonder that community shared agriculture is proliferating across North America.

Regional Community

It is crucial to end our reliance on the top-down, capital-intensive agribusiness that alienates communities from nature and forecloses the possibility of towns, cities and geographical areas taking care of their own food needs.

Strategies that are imposed on agricultural land from an office thousands of kilometres away cannot take into account local conditions and requirements. What is essential is an approach that attempts to understand the uniqueness of natural systems while forming a community with them. We need to shape human cultural behaviour to join with nature rather than to dominate and exploit it. Such an approach, philosophy, movement, attitude and practice goes by the name "bioregionalism."

While bioregionalism may sound like yet another "ism," it's been the easiest one ever for me to get used to and use. *Bio* has the same meaning of "life" as in biology (and as in the French word *biologique* which is the equivalent of our "organic"). The intent of bioregionalists is to ground human communities within natural regions, to encourage personal intimacy with specific geographic locales or territories in order to fit human behaviour to the Earth, rather than assume we can subdue the external world and get away with it.

In terms of sustainable agriculture, bioregionalism honours the diversity of crops and strategies appropriate to different ecosystems. Bioregionalism extends cooperation and mutual benefit to larger ecological systems. Yet the beauty and sanity of bioregionalism is its notion of operating within bounds that are both human and natural in scale. It incorporates a sense of containment and benign limitation beyond which solutions are too imposed, too large, too generalized, too insensitive and too inefficient. In its essence, bioregionalism is about taking care of home. By keeping our own patch of earth green, and respecting others' right to do the same, we may once again have a patchwork quilt that we are proud to call Earth.

The Community of the Garden

Gardeners are luckier than most people: gardens being a continual and multifaceted source of natural inspiration. Each garden dynamic is ever changing and demands an openness to being in the moment. We like to think we're in charge of garden events, but we're often reminded that there are many things we don't control. In truth, gardeners can influence growing conditions but it is not the gardener who grows the plant. The plant grows itself.

And there is a lot of other growing going on in the garden, including that of birds, bees, bugs and butterflies, all of which interact in myriad ways with both the garden and the gardeners. Growers who are open to recognizing and welcoming forces and energies beyond their limited selves become partners or co-creators of their garden. As such, they have the potential to manifest gardens that are uniquely different from those created by human will alone.

It took this gardener a while to slow wilful reactions to perceived threats to my garden. When a flock of Canada geese first started hanging around the farm, I came close to getting a dog to keep them away. They'd often be all over my beds. But I never caught them actually eating "my" seeds or plants, so I held off doing anything. Now there are over three dozen mostly permanent resident geese in Mansell Garden, and I gratefully acknowledge that they are one of my best sources of (purely organic, nitrogen-rich) fertilizer!

They've hit only two of my crops. Once they twice mowed down my kamut before it came back lusher than ever (thus confirming for me that kamut does have something more than ordinary wheats). And once they ate all my garbanzos just as the pods were swollen with green beans (thus teaching me that garbanzos at the green shell stage are a delicacy — something later confirmed for me by all the children selling them in the streets of Addis Ababa).

Similarly, I almost went ballistic when our five ducks started going under the fence and into the garden. It took me many months to drop my paranoia and become grateful to them for eating grubs, slugs and slug eggs.

Seeds of many of my plants have also taken to roaming around the garden. Many seem almost to be acting under specific directives from their parents, because when I hold back on commanding that they be only where I say, they end up creating eloquent new advertisements for themselves. Plant combinations and placements appear of which I would never have thought.

Every season I have more diverse plantings and every year the diversity of insects, birds and bees increases dramatically. As I've come to know some of the comings and goings of the life forms around me, I've grown to appreciate an intelligence I never expected, as well as a sense of humour and play. Social relations among all the communities in my garden are intricate, elaborate, brilliant and self-nourishing. Every year I wonder if things are getting too crowded for breathing space and every year the answer is, "Lots of room yet."

I'm not saying to simply let a garden find its own balance, or that there aren't lines to be drawn. To not fence a food garden from deer would be quite silly on Salt Spring Island, for example. But I have learned that it pays big time to recognize and respect the many communities that coexist in a garden. My own life has been enriched enormously as I've learned to be more cooperative, intuitive, watchful and open-hearted with all the lives that share my space. I'm an important player in the dynamic, ever-changing balance that results and everybody is on my team.

There's the life that you can see and there's also the life behind the life. People in many cultures revere all their relations with things of the Earth and, when growing or taking plants or animals for sustenance, communicate humbly, respectfully and thankfully with their essence or overlighting intelligence — the spirit of the plant or animal. I am not one of those gardeners who claims to be in actual and active communication with the devas and nature spirits, but I do believe we have a latent and unlimited ability to communicate and unite with nature's inner energies. And I do feel that such energies are another level of community that are working with and through me, even though I only sense them and am not consciously aware of them.

The times in which we live are unprecedented and demand very rapid change in the ways we inhabit this planet if we are going to continue to inhabit it at all. Strategies for safeguarding our food must address the following questions:

- Can we reverse the domination by the thoughts and values that have brought us to this place?
- Can we cease wilfully treating natural forms as subservient or irrelevant to us, and rekindle our appreciation and reverence for what already exists?
- Can we cease focusing so narrowly on the products of the world that we destroy the processes that produce them?
- Can we stop looking for more space and resources to exploit and instead regenerate and restore the spaces and renewable resources we still have?
- Can we can replace intense competition with continual cooperation, strong interaction and mutual dependence among life forms?

The garden, for me, is the place to start getting it all together. It is the first building block of health and sustainability as well as being a source of infinite inspiration and entertainment. If we can be community in our own gardens, we can move on to greater communities of neighbourhood, bioregion and globe. If we can grow to heartfully recognize, greet and listen to all of nature's beings in our own gardens, we can imagine and then create a garden on this Earth where all communities can live lightly on the land.

Seeding Seeds

Safeguarding our food can't happen if we don't safeguard our seeds. Seed saving is easy but we must now realize that no one is likely to do it for us in terms of the kinds of seeds we need for our ongoing nurturing. As with food, we can make a huge difference by acting together and saving seeds with friends, family, neighbours and community.

Some exciting avenues have already been created that are serving brilliantly to get our seeds back to where they once belonged, as a public resource.

Seedy Saturdays

One of those avenues comes with the code name Seedy Saturday. This annual seedy event, which usually happens on a Saturday in February or March, brings together all the people in a community who are excited by seeds. The first Seedy Saturday was in Vancouver, British Columbia, in 1990 and was the brainchild of Sharon Rempel and Roy Forster. Carolyn Herriot organized the second one in Victoria, British Columbia, in 1996. Since then Seedy Saturdays have cropped up in many communities, towns and cities across Canada. They are fun events that help preserve and enhance plant varieties that win accolades in any bioregion. They create an informal network of people who know what grows in an area and how to grow it.

It is very easy to organize a Seedy Saturday (or a Seedy Sunday or a Seedy Monday night ... or to have one after harvest, as well as one in spring). All you have to do is rent a hall, find a big living room or set up in a barn. Put up posters, run a story in the local paper, announce it at community meetings.

Every seed exchange that I've been to has a big swap table where people can easily look over the seeds that have been contributed, but one doesn't have to make a rule of this. Everybody with seeds can have their own table, or everyone can just walk around with their seeds, talking and trading.

It's helpful to have a classification system, such as signs indicating herbs, flowers, veggies, perennials, potatoes, garlic, et cetera. And it's good to have as much signage as possible about the seed offerings. Some people bring their seeds in packets with written descriptions and some people bring them in jars or bags. Remember to have lots of empty seed packets on the table as well as a few scoops and spoons.

Having knowledgeable volunteers at the exchange table makes things a lot more educational for neophyte growers. You can start and end at set times, but you can also wait until the group energy says it's time. My favourite seed swap is at Linnaea Farm on Cortes Island, British Columbia, where a potluck is combined with the seed trading: seed commerce is magically unannounced and can begin before, during or after eating.

Many Seedy Saturdays are large events, with tables representing gardening clubs, local seed companies, conservancy groups, alternative energy advocates and so on. Display tables can have seed-saving equipment and information. Catalogues of companies and organizations promoting open-pollinated seeds can be available for perusal. Beverages, snacks or meals can be made from locally grown heritage crops.

Participating in an annual seed exchange can alter your garden planning profoundly — as in, "Didn't Mary say she would bring her broccoli seeds again?" or, "How awesome that I will be spreading around the neighbourhood those vibrant calendulas that volunteer all over my own garden." Such exchanges enable you to carry the enthusiasm of the community along with your own garden enthusiasm.

Family, Friends and Neighbours

Family, friends and neighbours can swap seeds any time they want. They can trade lettuce and kale seeds just as they trade lettuce and kale. This is nothing new, but it could be happening a lot more. As gardeners realize they can save seeds and don't have to depend on seed companies for them, this empowered feeling will become contagious.

Friends and family can be nearby or far away for sharing seeds and the lore of the plants they produce. Every grower has personal favourites and every garden has different crops that usually grow the lushest. It's a natural way for highest-quality seeds to get around.

Trading seeds with your Aunt Thelma halfway across the country creates seed security in these weird years when one season can have record heat and another record cold. It means that she might be able to give you corn seed this time around, but it may be your turn to help her next. If Thelma's ex is also trading seeds with both of you, then it's even more likely that someone (and thus everyone) will have corn seed.

One of the great things about maintaining seed varieties among a circle of people is that, barring crop failures, you need only one member to grow lettuces, tomatoes or peppers to ensure everyone's seed supply. And such is nature's seed bounty that one lettuce, one tomato and one pepper from that one person theoretically could provide everyone's seeds, with some left over. When you consider that lettuce, tomato and pepper seeds easily stay viable for five years, it becomes obvious how simple it can be for a small group of people to keep lots of seeds alive.

As with Seedy Saturdays, there are many ways of organizing your exchanges, depending on who and where you are. You can visit each other, mail each other seeds for New Year, set it all up in conference calls, pass the word with e-mail, make a four-year plan, unite parts of the family here and there.

You could each have certain varieties for which you were responsible, or you could alternate. You could all be tomato seed savers. You could share zeal, do evaluations, make selections.

Some families, friends and neighbours are doing it already. Gardeners do it naturally. In our local post office, no one ever decided to make it happen; nevertheless six female employees have been trading fruits, vegetables, flowers, plants, cuttings and seeds for many years.

Seed Organizations

There are national seed organizations in Canada, the United States, Australia and some European countries that research, catalogue, preserve and distribute heritage seeds.

Having been involved with these groups over the years, and through selling old varieties through Salt Spring Seeds, I have observed recent changes in the meaning of "heirloom" or "heritage." For a while it was agreed that such seeds had to have been around for 50 years or more to merit the title. But now our entire heritage of seeds is being threatened by corporate seeds that you can't save. Until the 1990s, many excellent open-pollinated crops were developed by companies and governments working to actually improve crops (rather than make them resist herbicides or grow well with high chemical inputs). These cultivars are as worthy of saving as their older forebears and are coming to be included as heirlooms.

In the same context, it is important to note that the meaning of "hybrid" has changed as well. Fifty years ago, hybrids were the result of simple crosses that either happened spontaneously in nature or were facilitated by gardeners or researchers. Such hybrids were stabilized by growing them out over a number of seasons after which you could expect to get the same variety year after year by saving seed. Now "hybrids" refers to plant cultivars with parent lines controlled by plant breeders. Such varieties have not been stabilized and their seed is mostly worthless for seed-saving purposes. It is necessary to go back to the seed company for such hybrid seed.

So the seeds that you can obtain from heritage seed exchanges aren't necessarily very old, but they are all open-pollinated, i.e., non-hybrid, in the modern sense of the word. Seeds do come true and members are encouraged to save them. The vitality of seed organizations is dependent on the number of members not only growing out seeds but also re-offering them.

The seed savers organizations in Canada and the United States send all members an annual descriptive listing of who has seeds and who wants seeds. No fee is charged except to cover postage.

Through their publications, members of these groups learn not only about seed saving but also about heritage gardens and seed companies, as well as the stories of heirloom cultivars. These organizations maintain and formalize our living legacy of diverse plant resources, and their names and addresses are listed at the end of this book.

Seed Companies

Some companies in the United States and Canada still specialize in open-pollinated seeds. Salt Spring Seeds has traded seeds with many of these companies over the years and I have delighted in the spirit of openness and cooperation that has always permeated the exchanges.

In late 1999, a coalition of seed companies came together out of concern for the potential risks associated with the present use of genetic engineering. Member seed companies, including Salt Spring Seeds, endorse the following Safe Seed Pledge:

Agriculture and seeds provide the basis upon which our lives depend. We must protect this foundation as a safe and genetically stable source for future generations. For the *benefit of all farmers, gardeners and consumers who want an alternative, **we pledge that we do not knowingly buy or sell genetically engineered seeds or plants**. The mechanical transfer of genetic material outside of natural reproductive methods and between genera, families or kingdoms, poses great biological risks as well as economic, political and cultural threats. We feel that genetically engineered varieties have been insufficiently tested prior to public release. More research and testing is necessary to further assess the potential risks of genetically engineered seeds. Further, we wish to support agricultural progress that leads to healthier soils, genetically diverse agricultural ecosystems and ultimately people and communities.*

How likely are you to find genetically modified seed in a garden seed catalogue these days? Fortunately, the answer still is, "Very unlikely." This contrasts with the extreme likelihood of obtaining food products derived from gene-altered seeds. Most development and planting of bioengineered crops so far has been with corn, canola and soybeans. Vast acreages are being grown with these; you'll find it virtually impossible to find something in the supermarket that doesn't contain some form of them.

If you start seeing gene-modified seed in catalogues, it will be much more expensive than regular seed. We receive more than 30 catalogues annually and so far I've seen only the transgenic New Leaf potato offered. Just as you could tell your grocery store you'd prefer non-GMO foods, you could tell your favourite seed companies you'd be more likely to remain a customer if they didn't go in for biotech seeds.

Gardening Magazines

There used to be only two or three gardening magazines on our local newsstands but now there are two or three dozen. Quite a few of these have started providing a seed exchange section where subscribers list seeds they are offering or requesting.

Catching Seeds on the Internet

The internet is another medium that is coming on fast to proliferate our oldie-but-goldie seeds. There are all kinds of postings of seed exchanges, seed foundations, seed banks and seed custodians.

Seedy Individuals

Individual seed savers can and are making huge differences with their own initiatives. Farmers markets are great venues for turning people on to heritage seeds and plants. Grocery stores and markets can be persuaded to carry heirloom, open-pollinated plants. You can generate substantial income by being the one to grow these potted plants. Having descriptions and background as well as taste samplings with the plants adds to the excitement and to the sales.

Through the simple process of selecting for desired traits, plant lovers can improve our old cultivars. It used to be that seed companies did such selection as a matter of course and would rogue out plants that weren't high yielders, for example. But now seed companies are basically seed merchants that buy seed stock from the big boys who see little profit in improving simple, savable seeds. So it's up to us to enhance as well as maintain our seed stocks.

All these various and creative ways of honouring and cherishing our legacy of seeds! There is much going on in the world of seeds that is working toward a revivification of our daily meals, but a lot more needs to happen. This is what will work against the onslaught of terminator seeds and Frankenfood: people communicating with each other and sharing what is good.

Conclusion

In the six months since I began writing this book, the major biotech corporations have gotten more powerful and, to my mind, more outrageous. Do we really need grass that glows in the dark or men to birth babies? On the other hand, we have reason to be optimistic, as well. People are embracing "organic" much more significantly than they were even half a year ago.

In late December 2000, the U.S. Department of Agriculture, in reaction to some of the public protests that I mention in the foreword, issued new national standards for growing and processing organic food. One of the specifics was the banning of the use of biotechnology in organic produce.

It's easy to say that transnational corporations will take control of organics the way they have everything else. But if the organic rules outline that there be no genetically modified inputs, no synthetic pesticides, herbicides or fertilizers and that crops must be rotated, there is hope that the integrity of organic foods will not be compromised.

As a certified organic grower myself, I can attest to the honesty and seriousness with which organic certifiers enact their roles. I also am seeing that organic standards all across Canada are quickly becoming more articulated and sophisticated as organics really catch on.

Is it too late? Are the acres of genetically modified crops in North America already so vast that non-GMO crops are impossible to isolate and maintain as the foods we've known for thousands of years? Fortunately, the European nations have already shown that an educated public can turn things around on this issue and that it is still possible to say no to GMOs. But time is running out. It seems to me that a clear conclusion to the story of our food choices has to come within the next few years. If we keep allowing our choices to be made for us, soon there won't be any choices left.

We must cherish seeds as sacred vessels of the Earth's organic history. We must say no to the mad manipulation and mutilation of these seeds. Let us declare their right to be, as much as we declare our own right to be. Then seeds can flourish and yield glorious, future extravaganzas of healthy, whole food.

Further Information

Magazines and Periodicals

There are not many publications with a specific focus on organic methods and philosophy, but the following three are highly recommended:

Eco-Farm & Garden
Box 6408, Station J
Ottawa, Ont. K2A 3Y6
Website: www.cog.ca

Eco-Farm & Garden combines the best of what were previously *Cognition* and *Sustainable Farming* magazines.

Organic Gardening
Emmaus, PA 18099
U.S.A.
Website: www.organicgardening.com

Two excellent articles in *Organic Gardening* are "The Problem with Genetic Engineering," which appeared in the January/February 2000 issue, and "Our Food, Our Future" in the September/October 2000 issue.

Henry Doubleday Research Association
Ryton-on-Dunsmore
Coventry CV8 3LG
England

The best newsletter of food system analysis is put out monthly by Brewster and

Cathleen Kneen:

The Ram's Horn
S-12, C-11, RR 1
Sorrento, B.C. V0E 2W0
Website: www.ramshorn.bc.ca

Brewster's book, *Farmageddon: Food and the Culture of Biotechnology* (New Society Publishers, 1999), is the most in-depth history and examination of genetic engineering.

The book that best complements *The Whole Organic Food Book* is *Real Food for a Change*, by Wayne Roberts, Rod MacRae and Lori Stahlbrand (Random House, 1999).

Farm Folk, City Folk, by Herb Barbolet, Angela Murrills and Heather Pritchard (Douglas & McIntyre, 1998), is a favourite of mine for its stories, tips and recipes celebrating local food.

I recommend two books by Michael Ableman: *On Good Land: The Autobiography of an Urban Farm* (Chronicle Books, 1998) and *From the Good Earth: A Celebration of Growing Food Around the World* (Harry N. Abrams, 1993).

Among books on seed saving and plant breeding, three stand out for me: *Breed*

Your Own Vegetable Varieties: The Gardener's and Farmer's Guide to Plant Breeding and Seed Saving by Carol Deppe (Chelsea Green Publishing Company, 2000); *Seed to Seed: Saving Techniques for the Home Garden* by Suzanne Ashworth (Seed Saver Publications, 1991); and *The Seed Savers' Handbook* by Jeremy Cherfas, Michel and Jude Fanton (Grover Books, 1996).

Websites

The following websites are all excellent sources for current happenings in the world of genetic engineering:

Physicians and Scientists for Responsible Application of Science and Technology: www.psrast.org

Canadian Health Coalition: www.healthcoalition.ca

Union of Concerned Scientists: www.ucsusa.org/agriculture/biotech

Campaign for Food Safety: www.purefood.org/index

Rural Advancement Foundation International: www.rafi.ca

Council for Responsible Genetics: www.genewatch.org

Seed Companies and Seed Exchanges

Seed catalogues and seed exchanges continue to be crucial sources of information and inspiration for me. I especially look forward to receiving publications from the following each new gardening year:

Canadian Organic Growers
Box 6408, Station J
Ottawa, Ont. K2A 3Y6

Prairie Grown Garden Seeds
Box 118
Cochin, Sask. S0M 0L0

William Dam Seeds
P.O. Box 8400
Dundas, Ont. L9H 6M1

West Coast Seeds
8475 Ontario Street, Unit 206
Vancouver, B.C. V5X 3E8

Richters Herbs
Goodwood, Ont. L0C 1A0

Horizon Herbs
P.O. Box 69
Williams, OR 97544-0069
U.S.A.

Johnny's Selected Seeds
Foss Hill Road, RR 1, Box 2580
Albion, ME 04910-9731
U.S.A.

Abundant Life Seed
Foundation
P.O. Box 772
Port Townsend, WA 98368
U.S.A.

J. L. Hudson, Seedsman
Star Route 2, Box 337
La Honda, CA 94020
U.S.A.

Garden City Seeds
778 Highway 93 N
Hamilton, MT 59840
U.S.A.

Native Seeds/SEARCH
2509 North Campbell Avenue
#325
Tucson, AZ 85719
U.S.A.

Fedco Seeds
P.O. Box 520
Waterville, ME 04903-0520
U.S.A.

Bountiful Gardens
18001 Shafer Ranch Road
Willits, CA 95490
U.S.A.

Seeds of Diversity Canada
P.O. Box 36, Station Q
Toronto, Ont. M4T 2L7

Seed Savers Exchange,
3076 North Winn Road
Decorah, IA 52101
U.S.A.

HDRA Seed Library
Ryton Organic Gardens
Coventry CV8 3LG
England

The Seed Savers' Network
P.O. Box 975
Byron Bay, NSW 2481
Australia

Books

Excellent selections of mail-order gardening and ecology books are provided by the seed companies and exchanges listed above, as well as by the following:

The American Botanist
1103 West Truitt Avenue
Chilicothe, IL 61523
U.S.A.

Eco-logic Books
Mulberry House
19 Maple Grove
Bath BA2 3AF
England

Seeds for crops described in this book are available from Salt Spring Seeds, and I am always happy to answer gardening correspondence:

Salt Spring Seeds
P.O. Box 444
Ganges
Salt Spring Island, B.C.
V8K 2W1

Index